Dissertation Writing for Engineers and Scientists

PEARSON
Education

We work with leading authors to develop the strongest educational materials in engineering and science, bringing cutting-edge thinking and best learning practice to a global market.

Under a range of well-known imprints, including Prentice Hall, we craft high quality print and electronic publications which help readers to understand and apply their content, whether studying or at work.

To find out more about the complete range of our publishing, please visit us on the World Wide Web at: **www.pearsoned.co.uk**

Dissertation Writing for Engineers and Scientists

Student Edition

Mark Breach

Nottingham Trent University

PEARSON
Prentice Hall

Harlow, England • London • New York • Boston • San Francisco • Toronto • Sydney • Singapore • Hong Kong
Tokyo • Seoul • Taipei • New Delhi • Cape Town • Madrid • Mexico City • Amsterdam • Munich • Paris • Milan

Pearson Education Limited
Edinburgh Gate
Harlow
Essex CM20 2JE
England
and Associated Companies throughout the world

Visit us on the World Wide Web at:
www.pearsoned.co.uk

First published 2009

ISBN: 978-1-4058-7278-2

British Library Cataloguing-in-Publication Data
A catalogue record for this book is available from the British Library

Library of Congress Cataloging-in-Publication Data

Breach, M. (Mark)
    Dissertation writing for engineers and scientists / Mark Breach. – Student ed.
      p. cm.
    Includes bibliographical references and index.
    ISBN 978-1-4058-7278-2
    1. Research. 2. Engineering–Research. 3. Qualitative research. 4. Dissertations,
Academic–Authoriship. 5. Academic writing. I. Title.
    Q180.A1B74 2009
    808′.0665–dc22
                                                                  2008024591
10 9 8 7 6 5 4 3 2 1
12 11 10 09 08

Typeset in 9.75/12pt Galliard by 35
Printed and bound by Henry Ling Ltd., at the Dorset Press, Dorchester, Dorset

The publisher's policy is to use paper manufactured from sustainable forests.

Contents

List of tables

List of figures

List of boxes

Preface

Many university courses in science and engineering require their students to undertake a major project and write a dissertation upon it. The module associated with the project is often weighted as a double, triple or even bigger module. The prospect of undertaking a project can be very daunting to many students who, up to this point, have never embarked upon such a major exercise.

This book is written to help students at both undergraduate and postgraduate levels to understand, manage and excel at their own project and dissertation. The style is chatty and the book is designed to be an inspiring and informative text on this potentially dry subject. There are many short sections with headings to break up the text. Examples are presented in boxes and a summary and a list of action items are given at the end of each chapter.

The first chapter briefly explains the framework in which undergraduate and postgraduate projects and dissertations take place. It is written to reassure the student that although a project is probably the biggest piece of coursework they are ever likely to do, it is not a task to fear and evade. There is guidance on how to use the book while completing a project and on what the student should get out of a project.

The necessary skills and component parts of a project proposal are identified; rationale, question, aim, objectives, hypothesis, key questions, methodology, resources, structure, initial references, expected outcomes and work programme are all briefly introduced. The stages of the project process are described, namely the project proposal, presentations, initial literature review, the written dissertation, a journal paper and the viva. The role of the supervisor is considered and the reader is advised about maintaining a productive relationship.

Writing the project proposal is the most difficult and therefore daunting part of the whole process, but a well-crafted proposal will ensure success and a badly written one almost certain failure. The second chapter guides the student, who initially has absolutely no idea what to do, through the stages of selecting a suitable subject area that is of interest, forming a question and hence an aim, objectives etc. Different types of projects are considered, as are ways of adding value to make this substantial piece of work more rewarding.

Once the proposal has been submitted and accepted, the hard work begins. Although research methods are broadly categorised as qualitative or quantitative, in science and engineering it is mostly quantitative methods that are used. The nature of data is considered and experimental design, questionnaire design and the use and structure of interviews are considered. Almost all lead ultimately to some form of statistical analysis. The importance of designing for data collection and its subsequent analysis is emphasised.

While the project is being undertaken the student should also be writing it up. Guidance is given on how to approach the task as a whole and how to tackle each of the chapters in the dissertation. The importance of identifying the audience, keeping to the prescribed house style and the order in which to approach the component tasks are described. Citing references is covered in some detail.

Writing a dissertation is a major task and much can go wrong in the process. It is far better to plan to get it right and many tactics concerned with time and data management are described to ensure that all goes well. However, there is a reality that even with the best planning, disaster may strike. For example, if there are very few returns of a questionnaire, how should the student react? At least partial recovery is usually possible.

Finally the dissertation has been submitted. How will it be assessed and what lessons are there for the student to draw upon when writing the dissertation? How will other parts of the project such as the proposal and the viva be assessed? How should the student prepare for a successful viva?

Plagiarism is as big a sin in academia as cheating. It has always been easy to recognise that plagiarism has taken place; it has been much more difficult to prove it, therefore many tutors used to have an ambivalent attitude to the detection of plagiarism and the penalties for offenders. With electronic means of detecting the sources of plagiarised material, attitudes are hardening and the student needs to be aware of how to avoid accidentally committing this cardinal sin.

About the author

Mark Breach, is an experienced academic with many years of managing both undergraduate and postgraduate projects. He has been teaching Research Methods to MSc Civil and Geotechnical Engineers at Nottingham Trent University for several years and also teaches a similar course to undergraduates. As programme leader for the MSc course above, he manages all postgraduate dissertations and also performs a similar function for the undergraduates. He is also director of studies for PhD students working on programmes of study involving both science and engineering in Germany and Switzerland.

Mark Breach has an MA (Engineering, Experimental Psychology and Statistics) from Cambridge University, an MSc in Geodesy from Oxford University and a PhD in Geodesy (Nottingham Trent University). He is a fellow of the Royal Institution of Chartered Surveyors (RICS), the Royal Astronomical Society (RAS) and the Institution of Civil Engineering Surveyors (InstCES) and an Associate Fellow of the Royal Institution of Navigation (RIN). He is the author of many papers and books.

Acknowledgements

The author is indebted to his many students who, by undertaking their respective projects and dissertations, have contributed to the author's own understanding of the difficulties that students encounter.

Many staff at Nottingham Trent University, across a range of disciplines, have also helped by providing examples of good practice and I am particularly indebted to Dr Carl Brown, Dr Mark Davison, John Greenwood and Dr Carol Hall in this respect.

I am also most grateful to former students Anita Brealey, Seera Charavanamuttu, Chris Jackson, Paul Rushton, Dave Willmer and Tom Vajzovic, for permission to include some of their original project and dissertation work as examples.

Publisher's acknowledgements

We are grateful to the following for permission to use copyright material:

Figures 8.4 and 8.5 from the Turnitin UK website, www.nlearning.co.uk, Northumbria Learning Ltd.

In some instances we have been unable to trace the owners of copyright material, and we would appreciate any information that would enable us to do so.

CHAPTER

1

What is a dissertation?

1.1 Why do we do projects?

Scary isn't it?

You have made it through your degree so far, and the end is definitely in sight, but now you are faced with an apparently enormous hurdle. You have to do a project and write a dissertation on it. This looks like a much bigger task than any you have had to deal with before. You're right, it is. It looks daunting, it looks unmanageable, and in fact it looks downright impossible. Challenging it may be, but the key to making it manageable, and hence quite possible, is in understanding what is required and how to go about satisfying those requirements.

The purpose of this book is to show you how to do just that. By following the guidance here, along with the instructions you have received from your institution, you should be in the best possible position to write a top quality dissertation.

The aim of this chapter is to introduce you to the process of undertaking a project and writing a dissertation so that by the end of this chapter you should be able to:

- Understand how you can undertake an original investigation.
- Understand the difference between a project and a dissertation.
- Identify the component parts of a project.
- Recognise the importance of your tutor.

Keep this book handy as you work at your dissertation; you will need to refer to it time and again as you reach different stages of the work. There are many examples of 'how to do it' within the text and at the end of each chapter there is a bulleted summary of the main points. After you have finished this chapter it would be a good idea to have a look at all the other summaries to get an overview of what this book is about.

So knowledge, planning and preparation are the key words. You need to know what has to be done and hence plan how to do it. In any project, from painting a door to building a house, the key to success is all in the preparation and the same is true for your dissertation.

> **If you get the initial stages right the rest of the project, and hence the dissertation that you write, will follow easily.**

Why do your lecturers make you do a project? They are not being perverse or bloody-minded; there are some very serious objectives here. In most of your academic work you are required to learn specific facts or understand given ideas. You are then assessed upon your knowledge or understanding by reproducing the facts or applying the ideas in coursework or in examinations. In very little of this has there been the chance for you to decide for yourself what it is that you want to discover. There have been few opportunities to develop your own fresh ideas, or even to have any.

Projects and dissertations do just that; they allow you to take control of your learning and to develop the skills that can take you to a higher level of intellectual endeavour. So far you have been required to know facts and understand concepts and to apply that knowledge and understanding to solve particular problems. Now you have the chance to analyse, synthesise and evaluate – heady stuff indeed!

> **The research and writing skills you develop will also prepare you for the world of work.**

You will be asked to devise, manage and produce to a deadline a substantial piece of work. To do so you will have to draw upon extensive and deep knowledge of source materials to enable you to address a complex problem. You will have to demonstrate the research skills you have acquired. In doing this you will have to analyse and evaluate a wide range of appropriate and relevant data. You will need to show that you have understood the relationship between theoretical and practical studies.

Most importantly, you will need to express your own ideas on the matter under investigation. Finally you will need to communicate effectively the outcomes of your investigation to your tutors and peers, by means of a written dissertation and/or a written journal paper and possibly a presentation.

In most of the rest of this book we will assume that your written submission is to be a dissertation. If that is not the case and you are required to write a journal paper you will find that almost all the guidance for writing a dissertation also applies. There is specific guidance on writing for a journal in Section 7.7 'Preparing for publication'.

You will almost certainly be given a written instruction; alternatively it may have been placed on the web. Find out all the rules of the game before you start to play. For example, are there restrictions on the size of your dissertation; a minimum or maximum word count? What are the instructions about content, form and layout? What are the deadlines? Will your tutors read your draft work and comment or will they decline to do so? There is likely to be one tutor with specific responsibility for all the dissertations prepared by your course; find out who it is.

> **Make sure you understand, at an early stage, exactly what it is that your institution requires of you.**

Your ability to do a project and write up the dissertation is often taken as an indicator of your potential to undertake further education. A well-completed dissertation at undergraduate level, even if accompanied by indifferent marks in other subjects, will be viewed with favour when you apply to take a master's degree. If you apply to take a PhD, evidence of your ability to do research will be looked for in your master's dissertation.

Often, if your marks are on the borderline between classifications, an examination board will consider your performance in the dissertation to help it make a decision. A good project may pull you back from the brink of disaster, or propel you on to greater rewards.

As a frequent tutor of undergraduate and postgraduate projects the one thing that I really enjoy about projects is that I do not know what I am going to encounter when I start to read a particular dissertation. Marking students' work is usually one of the most mind-numbing of all academic duties. Try marking 100 essays on almost any topic and usually at least 95 of them will contain little more than a small subset of the material you have taught. Intellectually, it is a mighty tedious process.

> **For some, the biggest challenge is to avoid being overwhelmed by a task that has not been pre-planned for them.**

Dissertations, on the other hand, are quite different in that student authors take me on journeys of their own choosing. The most rewarding dissertations are those in which I learn something new from the student, and that happens often.

One of the most important criteria for your project is that your investigation must be original. Some eminent scientists have made their names by making high-profile advances in their fields of study; Kepler in planetary orbits, Newton in gravity, Darwin in evolution and Einstein in relativity, for example. You can discover new things too, perhaps not on such a grand or groundbreaking scale but certainly good enough to impress your supervisor as well as yourself.

> **So what can you do that *is* original?**

As a biologist you can investigate local distributions of flora and fauna in the field and draw conclusions on why these distributions change. As a civil engineer you can investigate management processes on the construction site by interview and question-naire with the personalities concerned. As a scientist in any field you can conduct experiments in the laboratory, for example to discover how properties of given materials are affected by different physical treatments. So doing something original may not be quite as difficult as you thought and you never know, you might just discover something really important.

The other side of the originality question is that of being tempted to take somebody else's work and write it up as if it were your own. This is plagiarism and will be considered by your tutors as a form of cheating. Do it and you are likely to fail, disastrously. There will be severe penalties for plagiarism and you risk being expelled from your institution.

Chapter 8 covers this serious business in more detail and, even as a student of the highest academic integrity, you should read this to ensure that you do not commit this sin by default.

Undertaking a project and writing the dissertation will develop a number of personal skills. You will need to plan your work extensively and manage your time effectively. You will have to apply existing knowledge to the problem in hand and in so doing you will have to exercise your skills of analysis, calculation, interpretation and evaluation.

You will have to solve problems and think creatively. It will be necessary to review and critically appraise existing literature upon your chosen subject. Depending upon your project you may need to take ethical and safety issues into account. Above all, you will have to work independently.

So, as a bottom line, what can you gain from doing a project and writing the dissertation that arises from it?

- A deep understanding of a new subject of your own choice.
- Impress your tutor who will then have something to draw on if you want a reference for your next job.
- Substantial evidence of your ability to work unsupervised and at an advanced level. That may impress a prospective employer.
- Extraordinary satisfaction from a job well done.
- There are often (monetary) prizes to be won. Talk to your tutors to find out the details.
- A good-looking book with which to impress your friends and family, particularly if your family has helped fund your education!

1.2 What is a project?

Each institution will conduct projects and dissertations in its own way. Even within a given institution different courses will manage dissertations differently so it is important that you understand what is required for your own work. In this book I will give general guidance that probably applies to your dissertation, but the instructions you have been given by your course management team should come first.

Firstly then, let's say what a project is not.

Your project is not an extended essay or a design exercise.

Merely collecting together all you know and can find out about a subject will be woefully short of the requirement. Likewise, a project is not a design exercise where you create plans for a new housing estate, turbine, tool or piece of scientific apparatus. An essential element of a project is that there should be some form of investigation where the outcome cannot be confidently predicted from the outset.

Your project is an investigation into something previously unknown, where the subject of your investigation is quite complex, relative to your current level of working. If you were working at PhD level then the essential requirement would be 'to make an original contribution to knowledge', i.e. to discover something that was not known by anyone before. This may not be something as dramatic or world-changing as discovering that $e = mc^2$ but nevertheless you should be capable of posing a new question and finding the answer to it – this represents your original contribution and it is as important as any other.

How do you start a project? The answer is with a question.

You need to discover a question relating to your favoured subject that does not have an immediate or easily found answer, but one for which an answer is probably possible. This may sound rather abstract at this stage, but do not worry, there are plenty of examples further on. Selecting the right question is the key to the success of your project but finding a suitable question is probably the hardest part of the process. However, be assured that having got this right, and you will, then the rest of the project, and hence the dissertation, will all flow from it.

Having found a question, the 'aim' of the project is then created by rephrasing that question. There should be just one aim for the project, so that the project is focused and narrow. If your aim has the word 'and' in it you probably need to think again. Too often projects are wide ranging and so become unfocused and rambling and also very difficult to bring to a conclusion in the finite time that is available.

> **It is usually better to have a project that is too narrow than one that is too broad.**

Having stated an aim you will then need to think about how you are going to satisfy that aim. This can be broken down into several related or unrelated activities and these become the 'objectives'. Now you know where you need to go, the next question to answer is: how are you going to get there? This is called the 'methodology' and you will need to figure out in some detail exactly what it is you are going to do. You need to ensure, before you start, that you have all the 'resources' necessary.

Having decided what it is that you are going to do, you will have some idea of what data you are going to collect. You should also decide what you are going to do with those data, i.e. how you are going to analyse them. Your level of knowledge of, and enthusiasm for, statistics will have a bearing here. With your numerical results and more importantly their analysis, you will then be in a position to draw some meaningful 'conclusions' and so make 'recommendations' as to how others may build upon your studies and hence start projects of their own to continue your work.

So here, in Figure 1.1, is the project process.

So there it is; how to do your project summarised in a few paragraphs. OK, there is rather more detail to consider. If there wasn't that would be the end of this book, but at least you now have a rudimentary skeleton on which to hang the flesh of your own project. Not so scary now, is it? Notice, however, that so far all this is mostly just about planning the task. With a well-thought-out and realistic plan you are much more likely to be successful than if you drift into the project with some vague hope that all will turn out right in the end.

1.3 What happens when?

Your project will take place over a period of time which will vary from course to course. You will probably receive some written instructions and guidance from your course management and you should read this carefully to ensure that you understand what is required from you at each stage of the process. You may be given a list of subjects that your tutors would like investigated, possibly in support of their own research, but this

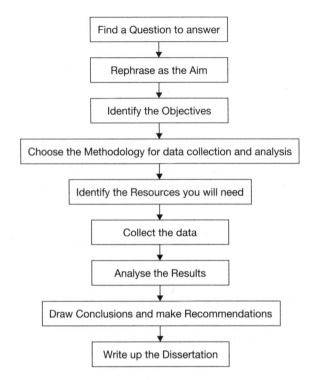

Figure 1.1 Outline of project process

method of subject selection is becoming less favoured in some institutions as it takes away your initiative even before the process has started. On the other hand, some tutors recognise that many students need more help to get started.

There is a brief example of a project list in Box 1.1 where a short description is given for each project. Some projects will be more practical and some more theoretical and you should evaluate what is on offer in the context of your own abilities. If you have to choose from a list, find out if the project can be adapted to your own special interests.

If you select a topic from a list, it is vital that it is one you are enthusiastic about. In preparing lists of projects some tutors may be inviting you to participate in their own research. This can be exciting but you must make sure that you can produce a well-rounded dissertation from the project that you are offered and you are not just going to be used as a laboratory technician by the tutor. Also make sure that you will be capable of and willing to do the work that is asked of you.

Often you will be asked to propose your own project and will be required to formalise that proposal in a 'project proposal', sometimes called a 'project definition document'. In the rest of this chapter we will say more about the project proposal document.

> **A project proposal is the planning document in which you set down on paper your ideas for conducting the project.**

Box 1.1 Example of part of a project subject list

Project suggestions

Encouraging roots to penetrate deeply (with J.G.)
Vegetation may be used to reinforce soil slopes and reduce the risk of slope instability. You will assess the strength of different plant roots, and develop techniques to encourage deeper penetration into the ground.

External ballistics (with C.B.)
A projectile in free flight experiences an aerodynamic drag force that depends on the density of the medium in which it is travelling, its velocity, its cross sectional area, and a factor called the drag coefficient. The drag coefficient is determined predominately by the profile of the projectile in the direction of travel. Experimental measurements will be performed to investigate the magnitude of aerodynamic drag on various projectiles and shapes of projectiles using one or more of the following experimental systems: (i) terminal velocity when falling under gravity in a viscous fluid, (ii) the actual horizontal range or vertical height of a projectile fired by a mortar compared to the theoretical maximum values in a vacuum, (iii) the force on a stationary object in a moving airstream, and (iv) the decrease in velocity of a pellet from a BB gun as a function of distance.

Did Scott and Amundsen really find the South Pole? (with M.B.)
History glosses over how close they really were; they used the imperfect survey and navigation instruments of their time. Obtain copies of their original astronomical observations at the South Pole and recompute the original observations by rigorous means with precise celestial data to find out how close they really were. You will need a willingness to learn some navigational astronomy and the tenacity to track down and interpret the original data.

Effective dowsing (with F.C.)
Dowsing is an ancient art for finding things like water, metal ores or even lost keys. There are no really scientific explanations of why it works, but for some people it appears to work very effectively. Some believe that underground services, hazards, watercourses, archaeological structures and other significant features can be detected by this ultimate low-tech, and therefore cheap, method of dowsing. Devise experiments to find out who can do it and how well.

Rainwater harvesting (with M.D.)
Investigate the various techniques for harvesting natural rainwater and the potential usage that such water could be put to in order to supplement the general water supply in areas that suffer from water shortages.

The effect of recent British weather on wildlife (with P.P.)
Summers are becoming unpredictable and extreme; hot and dry one year, wet and windy the next. Plants and animals are under stress. Investigate the evidence to see whether climate change is significantly affecting animal behaviour.

You will probably have a short series of lectures about projects to get you off to a good start. It is vital that you attend all of these lectures as you will get a lot of useful detail and guidance on how to do all the different steps of your project. Experience shows that there is a strong correlation between your attendance at these lectures and your final grade for the dissertation.

Some institutions start the project process in the previous year to encourage and enable students to think about what they are going to do before the final academic year starts. Those students that actively engage at this stage are usually the ones that produce the best dissertations.

It is likely that you will be allocated a tutor who will be one of the staff in your university. That person could be an expert in the subject that you are intending to investigate, but even if not an expert, should be knowledgeable about how to conduct a project, and that is probably more important. If you are a part-time student and are working in industry you may also have an industrial tutor who knows your subject area well.

> **Getting the best out of your tutor will definitely enhance your chance of success.**

Your tutor is there to keep you on the academic 'straight and narrow' so that you do yourself justice by completing the project to the best of your capabilities. There is more about your tutor in Section 1.5.

Apart from writing a project proposal there may be one or more of the following milestones to pass, some or all of which may be formally assessed, so make sure you are aware of all of the requirements.

A 'literature review' is an investigation into what is already known about the subject. There is no point in starting out in ignorance, doing some very hard and detailed work just to 'reinvent the wheel'. It is pointless and simply not clever and you will get little if any credit for it.

Whatever you do, it will build on the work of others just as the likes of Einstein, Brunel and Rutherford built upon the work of others in their respective fields. The literature review will be a substantial portion of your dissertation so you may be required to produce a small one early on to make sure you have got the idea of how to do it. I will take you through how to write a literature review in Chapter 5.

If your project takes place over a long period or even a whole year, your course leaders may require you to report your progress by stages. These may be by way of monthly reports in which you detail your progress so far. You may be required to report:

- Activity or achievements since the last report
- Meetings or other contact with tutor(s)
- Your proposed actions before the next report
- A list of the obstacles inhibiting your progress and your ideas on how to overcome them.

Alternatively, or as well, you may be asked to make presentations to your tutor and fellow students in which you may:

- Give a brief introduction to and explanation of the subject
- State its formal aim and objectives
- Describe the methods that you have used in your investigation so far
- Show any results that you might have obtained so far
- Describe the problems facing you and how you intend to resolve them.

Remember the level of your audience's knowledge and do not go into unnecessary complexities that only you are familiar with. Do not worry if, as yet, you have few results to tell your audience about; after all, your project is far from complete. Your time for the presentation will probably be quite limited so make sure you have a plan of what you are going to say. You will have to grab your audience's attention, so make sure you have something interesting to tell them. Details are unimportant at this stage; it is the overview that is required.

The purpose of this presentation is to make sure you are on the right track and that you are making acceptable progress. Your lecturers know that many students who work only to the next deadline will be seriously impaired if they try to treat the project in the same way. It is simply too big an enterprise to be undertaken so lightly.

The next formal deadline is likely to be that of handing in the dissertation. Make sure you know well in advance where and when this is to be. Find out the required format for the text and layout and the correct form of binding. Writing up the dissertation is covered in Chapter 5.

> **There are usually severe penalties for late submission.**

Your tutor and perhaps others now have the pleasure of reading and assessing your submission. There is nothing you can do now but be on hand and alert to your emails in case they have any queries. Once your dissertation has been read there may be a viva voce, i.e. an examination by word of mouth. This will be in the form of a presentation by you followed by questions from your examiner(s). There are more details on the assessment process in Chapter 7.

● 1.4 Planning the project

To plan your project you will need to write a 'project proposal'. This will probably be quite short, but will be a very important document. Your institution will tell you what is required but it will probably be under similar headings to those in Table 1.1.

Completing a project proposal is a substantial task, so do not leave it until just before the deadline for submission. The proposal may only be a few pages long but, if done well, will reflect many hours of detailed thought. How you write the project proposal is covered in the next chapter. You are unlikely to be able to complete the whole document

Table 1.1 The project proposal

Your details	Name, course and contact details.
Title	The proposed title of your project. At this stage it will be just a working title which may be revised as the project develops.
Rationale	You need to give a brief statement as to why you've chosen the topic. If you are a part-time student in employment, show how it relates to your employer's needs. How brief this section will be depends upon the instructions from your institution. It could be quite lengthy if you are required to include a critical appraisal of existing literature here.
Question	This is the question that you are seeking to answer.
Aim	Your formal statement of the aim.
Objectives	You should write a clear set of three to five brief statements of your specific objectives. They need to be achievable and measurable. When all of them have been completed the aim of the project will also have been achieved.
Hypothesis	A hypothesis is a statement of an idea that may or may not be true. If you have a working hypothesis you will be seeking to support or deny it. A hypothesis is not appropriate for every project and you should decide if it is suitable for yours.
Key questions	You may have some important questions of specific detail that you need answers to. If so, list them here. Key questions are not appropriate for every project.
Methodology	In this section you need to describe how you are going to conduct your investigation. Include details of the data you need to collect and where you expect to get them from. You also need to give some details of the method of statistical analysis that you will use. This will allow you to present results that have meaning and hence draw conclusions from those results.
Resources	List all the resources that you will need to complete your project. This will include the hardware you need for any experiments or fieldwork, the software for data processing and analysis, the human resources you will call upon for interviews or technical help. State how you are going to get all these resources.
Structure	At the very least this will be a list of chapter headings for your dissertation. Although you probably do not have an exact idea of what your finished dissertation is going to look like at this stage, you should try to give chapter subheadings where you can.
Initial references	It rather depends on what has gone into your rationale above. If the rationale is very brief then it is likely that you will be required to list the references that you have consulted so far and so intend to use when you undertake your literature review. If your rationale includes at least a partial literature review then this section is the list of references that you have cited in the text. How to undertake a literature review and how to cite references are described in Chapter 5.
Expected outcomes	Try to predict your possible results. This will inform your choice of working hypothesis and you may now want to go back and revise it.
Work programme	Your work programme may be a bar chart, often called a Gantt chart, or a series of key events with target dates.

at one sitting but if it is in a word-processing file you will be able to return to it from time to time to add further details.

1.5 Your tutor, friend or foe?

Your tutor is probably neither, but is certainly a 'resource' that you should use to best advantage. If you can get your tutor sympathetically on your side then you have a powerful ally, especially if your tutor is also the person who marks your dissertation. How your tutor is allocated to you will vary from institution to institution. You may just have someone allocated to you, or you may be able to express a preference, or you may even be able to select the person of your own choice. If either of the last two applies to you, consider your choice with care. The most easygoing or the most popular member of staff may not necessarily be the best one for you.

What you want from your tutor is support and guidance. You need to agree the frequency and format of meetings and having done so, stick to that agreement. Nothing annoys busy professionals more than preparing and making themselves available for a meeting to find that the student fails to turn up without notice or explanation.

> **Your tutor will be much more impressed if you come well prepared to the meeting and so keep it productive, focused and if possible, short.**

To keep your tutor on your side, make sure you inform your tutor of your progress, ask for advice, ask if your progress is satisfactory and discuss your future action plans. Your tutor will almost certainly make comments that are uncomfortable to hear. Accept criticism gracefully; it is for your own good and you will produce a better dissertation for it. You are likely to get more marks if you follow your tutor's guidance.

It is a good idea to keep a simple record of meetings with your tutor, partly to remember what was agreed and partly to have evidence that the meetings took place. This might be useful if your tutor becomes ill or leaves the institution and a new tutor is assigned. Figure 1.2 shows a simple form that you might use.

If you are a part-time student working in industry with an industrial tutor, make sure your tutor has a copy of any guidelines or instructions that you have been given and also the contact details of the appropriate lecturer at your institution. Industrial tutors are often unsure of what is expected of them, especially if they are asked to assess your work formally.

If you have the opportunity to do so, how will you select the right tutor for you? Obviously it needs to be someone you get on with and trust. Try to select a person who is likely to be with you for the whole of your project. Someone about to retire, overly ambitious or disenchanted with their job may best be avoided. A subject expert in the area of your project would be nice but someone knowledgeable in the requirements of projects and dissertations would normally be better, especially at undergraduate level.

If you are a part-time student you might be considering asking your boss. If so, that might make your boss more amenable to giving you access to resources and time off to complete the work, but it might also create conflict of interest situations. If you make a good job of the project you will shine; a bad result could be very negative.

Above all, you would like a tutor who is accessible, sympathetic and tolerant.

Supervision meeting date

Who is present

Brief notes of the main points of discussion:

Review of action items at the last meeting

   1.

   2.

     ...

Agreed actions from this meeting including due date

   1.

   2.

     ...

Signed (student) ....   Signed (tutor) ....   Date ....

Figure 1.2 Supervision meeting record

This chapter has been just an introduction to projects and dissertations but you should now have a good idea of what is required of you and what you have to do. Before jumping ahead and starting your project, at least review the chapter summary below and skim through the rest of this book. Obviously, as you come to each of the stages listed in the chapter headings and subheadings in the contents list, read the appropriate sections carefully.

● 1.6 Summary

- A project is not an extended essay or a technical design exercise.
- Read your institution's instructions and guidelines; then follow them exactly.
- Take the time and care to get your project proposal right.

- Start your project with a question seeking an answer.
- Then develop the aim, objectives and methodology.
- Plan how you will process the data to get valid results and conclusions.
- Keep your tutor 'on board'; prepare for meetings and always turn up on time.
- Your potential for the next level of education will be heavily influenced by the quality of your dissertation.
- The most rewarding dissertations are those where the tutor also learns something new.

What next?

Read the summary bullet points and 'What next?' sections from all the other chapters in this book. Skim through the rest of the text.

Get a copy of your institution's instructions and read it twice.

Put all the deadlines into your diary.

Attend all lectures, tutorials and seminars for the project/dissertation that your course runs. They are there for a reason.

Find out who your tutor is and discuss your ideas, no matter how vague or tentative they are at this stage.

CHAPTER
2

Making a start

2.1 Choosing and defining the project

So now you are ready to make a start.

The first step is to decide what specific subject you want to do your project on. This can be a difficult decision. In Chapter 1 the 'question', 'aim', objectives', 'hypothesis', 'methodology' and 'resources' were all mentioned and each of these will need to be carefully examined. But before you even get that far you need to select a subject that you wish to investigate.

It is vital that you choose a subject that inspires you. Motivation is essential. This is going to be your own independent piece of work so you should be driven from within. Nobody is going to be constantly on your back telling you what to do next. The bottom line is that *you* are in charge.

The aim of this chapter is to help you to identify and plan a suitable project and write the proposal. By the end of this chapter you should be able to:

■ **Identify a subject that really interests you.**

■ **Understand the different types of project that you may undertake.**

■ **Plan a project.**

■ **Write a project proposal.**

There are various ways to select a suitable project. You might get ideas by reading books or papers associated with your lectures or when you are doing coursework. You may be inspired by experiments or investigations you have done in the laboratory or in the field. Perhaps you can draw on your own experience, particularly if you have worked on a summer job or sandwich placement in industry.

Maybe you have some ideas already or maybe your mind is a complete blank and you have absolutely no idea how to proceed. Let's assume the latter. Here is one way, but not the only way, of selecting a topic. In this method identify those aspects of your

Table 2.1 Selection of a general area for your project

Subjects I really like	Subjects I am so-so about	Subjects I absolutely hate
Surveying	Public health science	Geology
Mathematics	Fluid mechanics	Geotechnics
Numerical analysis	Highway engineering	Masonry design
Structural analysis	Construction	Materials
Structural design	Mechanics	Soil mechanics

course that you like and those that you do not. Make a list. It does not have to be based upon the module titles but that is one way of doing it. Table 2.1 lists the modules on a particular course that the student has ranked for enjoyment. Your course will be different; this is just to illustrate the process.

Now focus on the subjects you really like. Mathematics and numerical analysis are support subjects, as are information technology and communication skills. It is unlikely that, in the context of any science or engineering subject, they will lead you directly to a suitable project. So, in the example above, the choice is narrowed to surveying, structural analysis or structural design.

Let us assume that, of those subjects, it is surveying that fires you up the most. Now ask yourself what it is about surveying that grabs your attention; perhaps repeat the exercise looking at the subject sub-headings of surveying as in Table 2.2.

At this stage you would probably consider what it is about the subject that you really like; in our example, it is the Global Positioning System (GPS) or setting-out. For example, if it was GPS, do you wish to investigate some aspect of the technology of GPS itself or to investigate the feasibility of a proposed novel application? If you had a passion for the sport of mountain biking, you might want to find out how GPS can help you develop your performance in competition.

You might also consider if there is an interface between your favourite subjects that is worthy of investigation, e.g. 'what are the best methods of using GPS for setting-out?' If there was such a connection, you would suddenly find that you are on to the next stage, the question.

But before you go too far, a short reality check is called for. Is this really going to be a feasible project? You need to read extensively around the subject to find out what others have thought about it before.

Table 2.2 Selection of a specific area for your project

Surveying subjects I really like	Surveying subjects I am so-so about	Surveying subjects I absolutely hate
Global Positioning System	Laser scanning	Digital photogrammetry
Setting-out	Geographical Information systems	Cadastre
	Remote sensing	
	Geodesy	

> **Read articles in academic and professional journals and see what you can find about your chosen subject on the internet.**

This will help you to narrow the subject further. There is always a balance to be struck between going for too broad a subject in which you lose direction and ultimately present a muddled and superficial dissertation and too narrow a subject where you are unable to find anything that others have written on it before.

Discuss your ideas with your tutors at an early stage. You may get help or inspiration from them. Just talking about your ideas will help to sort out the bad ones from the good ones.

> **An alternative approach to finding an interesting project is to start by identifying a general topic area and then looking for the problems, opportunities and questions within that area.**

You can do this by reading research literature associated with the subject. Next identify potential solutions and focus on one or more of these to create your research question.

It may be that you really have identified something that no one has ever investigated before; if so, well done! You could be on to a winner. More likely you will identify something that has been only incompletely investigated. For example, if you find out about one investigation that was limited by time or place or only some of the possible variables were considered, you may be able to replicate that investigation at a different time or place etc. Or you might investigate the same thing but in a different way. You will then be able to compare and contrast your results with those of the original investigation.

Ask yourself if you are going to be able to get the necessary technical information or the opinions of others that you need. Will there be issues of commercial confidentiality that will make others unwilling to cooperate? Find out what the situation is in your institution regarding confidentiality issues in relation to sensitive material in your dissertation. It may be that by submitting your dissertation you are agreeing that it will automatically be put into the public domain. If issues of confidentiality present an insurmountable problem you may need to find another subject to investigate.

● 2.2 Motivation and added value

Motivation was mentioned earlier. You can enhance your motivation by adding value to your project in a number of ways. It is not essential that you do so, but it may spur you on that little bit extra.

If you are a part-time student in employment, consider if the subject you intend to investigate would lead to something useful for your employer. If so, then your employer might give you extra support such as technical resources or even paid time to develop your ideas.

Some professional institutions and commercial companies may provide financial support for students undertaking specific projects. Seek advice from your tutor and see any appropriate websites.

> To enhance your motivation consider whether:
>
> ■ Your project is useful to your present or future employer?
>
> ■ You can get financial support from a professional institution?
>
> ■ You can interest a commercial company in providing technical support to develop your ideas?
>
> ■ You could publish a paper when the dissertation is complete?

You are going to write a substantial dissertation. Will it be possible to use all or part of it to write a paper for publication in an academic or professional journal, or possibly even a book? This may sound a bit ambitious but every author starts somewhere. Your submission does not have to be groundbreaking. Even modest ideas in short articles may be acceptable for publication. If you get into print it will look good on your CV and give you initial exposure within your chosen industry. If you intend to become an academic, publications are what careers are built on.

2.3 What type of project?

Most projects fall into one of three broad categories:

■ practical investigation;

■ review or critical commentary; or

■ opinion or attitude survey.

A practical investigation will normally involve laboratory work or fieldwork and will usually be of an experimental nature. You will need to devise experiments or plan a field campaign to discover or deduce relationships between selected parameters. It is likely that you will have plenty of numerical data and that you will use statistical methods to draw statistical inferences from those data. This in turn will lead you to conclusions based upon measured probabilities.

Examples

■ In an investigation into the use of colliery spoil as fill, one objective is to find the relationship between compaction results from the laboratory tests of colliery spoil and field trials of colliery spoil placed in situ.

■ In an investigation into the accuracies that can be obtained using GPS in conjunction with the Ordnance Survey's 'Active GPS Network', GPS observations for different periods of time were processed with different limitations of time, meteorological data and satellite ephemeredes to find the optimum observing conditions to achieve given accuracy requirements.

One variant of the practical type of investigation is the software development project and that will be considered later.

A review or critical commentary will be of a process or technique that is relevant to your area of study. The difficulty with such a project is that there is the danger that it will be little more than a grand literature review backed up with case studies. It is very hard to show originality of thought in such a dissertation.

You will need to do a substantial evaluation of the process or technique under investigation and you will need to introduce a significant number of your own justified ideas and opinions to demonstrate your own input into the dissertation. Your project should penetrate the topic in a critical way, allowing you to come to reasoned conclusions; not just review or summarise an area of knowledge.

Examples

■ In an investigation into the shallow lay of water mains the researcher investigated the existing techniques and legislation relating to buried water mains and critically reviewed alternative approaches with respect to the economics, environment, risks, political and social issues.

■ In an investigation into the derivation of generic assessment criteria for human health in response to the risks posed by land contaminated with polychlorinated biphenyls (PCBs), the researcher identified that there was no published soil guideline value report for PCBs and so investigated how to derive generic assessment criteria.

A survey involves collecting other people's ideas or opinions and usually takes the form of questionnaires and/or interviews. For this type of project to be successful you need to give considerable thought to designing and focusing the questionnaires and interviews to ensure that you get plenty of the questionnaires returned. You will need to think carefully about how the information you get back will be processed and how you will be able to draw meaningful conclusions from it.

Examples

■ In an investigation into Geosynthetic Reinforced Road Embankments the investigator used interviews with practitioners to gather opinion on the need for using geosynthetic reinforced systems in road embankment construction in Ghana.

■ In an investigation into passive solar architecture the investigator used questionnaires to find out opinion about the desirability and practicality of using passive solar heating for buildings in the UK.

2.4 What is the question?

Deciding the question that you seek to answer is the most critical part of your project. Get this right and everything will flow out from it. Get it wrong and you may find yourself up against all sorts of difficulties. It is very hard to say what a good question is. It really comes down to a balance of judgement, trial and error, luck and inspiration.

It should not take you long to realise whether you are onto a winner or a lemon.

By following the process of developing your aim, objectives, methodology, resources and analysis of data in order, it will soon become apparent whether you have a viable project or not. If you find yourself going up a blind alley, go back to the start point and try a different route.

The process of finding a suitable question starts with defining your project area, as we did at the beginning of this chapter. For example, if your interest was in GPS to enhance competitive mountain biking performance then your question might be:

> **Question**
>
> How can GPS be used to enhance competitive mountain biking performance?

It is as simple as that.

Here is another example from a physics project.

> **Question**
>
> How does a droplet evaporate on a super-hydrophobic surface?

2.5 The aim

The aim comes directly out of the question. It is just a case of rephrasing the question into the form: 'the aim of this project is to (investigate) . . .'. In our GPS-biking example this will become:

> **Aim**
>
> The aim of this project is to investigate the use of GPS for enhancing competitive mountain biking performance.

If this last bit of text looked repetitive, it is. All that has happened is that the question has been rephrased. Note the use of the word 'investigate'; this is a strong word in dissertations. The aim should be simple, single and focused, and above all, achievable.

Here is the aim of the physics project.

> **Aim**
>
> The aim of this project is to investigate how a droplet evaporates on a super-hydrophobic surface.

For a software development project the aim will be to solve a specific problem.

● 2.6 The objectives

The objectives are those steps that you need to go through to satisfy your aim. Obviously there will need to be a literature search at the beginning and once you have some results there will be analysis leading to conclusions and recommendations. However, since these will apply to every project we will gloss over them here.

> **The objectives list those actions or sub-investigations that need to be undertaken to make it possible to achieve the aim.**

The number of objectives depends upon the project, but three to five is likely to be a good number. Any less, then it is probable that either the project is too trivial or that you are considering it in insufficient detail. If you have significantly more than five then you may have difficulty in achieving them all in the time you have available. If you have too many objectives, consider narrowing your aim.

In our GPS-biking example the objectives might be:

Objectives

1. To determine what geometric and biometric parameters of mountain biking performance you need to investigate and how knowledge of them can be used to aid overall individual performance.

2. To find out which GPS receivers are suitable for installation on a mountain bike/rider and will work satisfactorily in the mountain biking environment.

3. To find out whether, and how, GPS can help you to investigate your chosen parameters and so decide what other sensors or technology you may need and how they will be integrated into your project.

4. To undertake a field trial to investigate the effectiveness of your chosen technology configuration and so improve upon your ideas.

Here are the objectives of the physics project.

Objectives

1. To find out how super-hydrophobic surfaces are created through the method of the patterning of copper surfaces by etching through a mask.

2. To investigate the mechanism of evaporation of deionised water on those surfaces.

3. To develop and investigate a new method for the creation of super-hydrophobic surfaces by copper electrodeposition.

2.7 Methodology

The methodology section is about deciding how you are going to achieve your objectives. At each stage examine what you propose to do to make sure it is possible, necessary and realistic. You should rigorously consider the data you need to collect: what type; how much; and with what precision.

More importantly, consider what you are going to do with the data when you have got them, i.e.:

■ how you are going to analyse them;
■ what statistical tests will be applied;
■ what level of statistical confidence you will require from your results.

This in turn will tell you how much data you need to collect and with what precision. So you can now revise your earlier ideas on this matter. Sometimes this may not be possible but, if you cannot revise your ideas, then you run the risk of using only the data that you have collected and having to make the most of whatever analysis you can do.

Any fieldwork should be planned to ensure that the analysis and conclusions drawn from it are robust and can be defended. To achieve this you would, invariably, want to conduct more extensive field trials or laboratory work than you have the time or resources to do. Therefore your results are unlikely to be as strong as you would like them to be. If this is so, then that should be reflected in your commentary upon the limitations of the project.

> **Every project has its limitations.**

Every project has its limitations and you should acknowledge them; it will give your examiner more confidence in your scientific rigour if you do.

It may be that your methodology includes one or more case studies. Beware of over-reliance upon case studies because if you are merely reporting upon work that has been done by others there may be little input into the discussion by yourself and this will be obvious to your examiners.

> **A single case study may give significant insight, but that will be only into the case you are studying.**

It is unlikely that you will be able to draw any general and therefore more meaningful conclusions from a single case study. Comparing and contrasting factors from several case studies is much more likely to be productive.

On the other hand, there are some disciplines where a single case study is appropriate, where the intention is find out about aspects of that case. When investigating an animal behavioural problem a single case study may give insight to the cause of that behaviour.

Lecturers often use case studies to illustrate teaching points. If you are using case studies it will be because you are researching into those specific cases. Each case study should be set in the context of prior studies into comparable cases.

You may think that case studies are a useful way of padding out a weak and rather thin project, especially if you have a handy technical report you obtained while working in industry. This is true but, again, your examiners will spot it at once and will almost certainly mark you down for it. If you are drawing heavily on one source for your case study be extra careful that you do not open yourself to a charge of plagiarism and all the consequences that may bring; see Chapter 8.

Let's now return to the GPS-biking example above; your thinking about the methodology might run like this.

Methodology

In **objective 1** you need to find out just what it is that you have to investigate to improve your biking performance. If your sporting objective is to get around a given course in the least time then measurements of time, position, speed and acceleration are obviously important and GPS should be able to help you here.

If you are looking to see how your body is affected by your performance and vice versa then you will need to find out about measuring heart and breathing rate and other biometric parameters that are investigated in sports science.

Now it is time for a reality test. Do you know, or can you find out, enough about the science or engineering aspects you are currently not familiar with? If you are a sports scientist, what do you know about GPS data processing? If you are a surveyor, what do you know about sports science methods? Do you have access to the necessary technologies? If not, then go back to the objectives, aim, question, or the selection of the subject stage and reconsider your options.

For **objective 2** you would need to find out what GPS receivers and software were available. You may be practically constrained by the GPS receivers that your institution has or you may have access to GPS technology from other sources such as companies you have contacts with. If you intend to spend your own money, budget for everything before you start.

There are many GPS receivers and software packages on the market with a range of capabilities and limitations and at greatly different prices. Make sure that what you eventually use is suitable for the task in hand. Consider the limitations of the application of your chosen technology; in our example ask yourself if your chosen GPS set will record data whilst being jolted by every rock the bike hits and if the receiver will pick up satellite signals when biking through woods. So, to satisfy objective 2, you need to identify some suitable technology. Reality test: can you get the GPS technology you need?

In **objective 3** you will need to consider how GPS at the available level of precision for time, position, speed and acceleration can give you the data you need to enable you to improve your biking performance. You will need to state how any other biometric sensors will be linked to the GPS data; through a common time scale perhaps.

Now to the most difficult part: decide how the data you collect are to be processed and analysed and how they may be used to enhance biking performance. It may not be possible to do that definitively just yet, so you may need to conduct a small pilot study to find out just what you can get out of your proposed data. This in turn will tell you something about the methodology you will need to use to satisfy objective 4.

Here is a methodology for the physics project.

> **Methodology**
>
> In **objective 1** you need to establish the different stages for the creation of super-hydrophobic surfaces from normal copper samples, with or without photoresist. Spin coating may be the best way. Clean the samples with deionised water and acetone before applying photoresist. Determine the coating by setting the spin rate. Soft bake the layer and expose to ultraviolet radiation through a mask. Develop the pattern with a PCB developer. Etch using a brawn solution and check for quality. Create the hydrophobic layer with Granger's water-based fluorochemical.
>
> For **objective 2** you would need to deposit droplets with a range of radii onto the substrate. Record the evaporation of the droplet with a video camera. Control scale by not adjusting focus. Measure the contact angle and radius using image analysis software. Compute estimated errors.
>
> In **objective 3** you will need to deposit copper on the surface by copper plating using a copper acid bath.

For a software development project the methodology may include flowcharts or design diagrams. You will need to explain how the software will be broken down into small blocks for development, and what procedures you will use to test the functionality of the component parts. If the software is to be tested as a case study the test process should be described, including the data that are to be captured. If the software is to model a physical problem then analytical models should be devised to test the program against.

● 2.8 Hypothesis and key questions

A hypothesis is a working assumption that is to be tested. It should of course be sensible and may be something that is generally assumed but for which there is little concrete evidence. It may indeed reflect a long-held but popular prejudice. Not every project has to have a hypothesis; it depends entirely on whether it is appropriate in your particular case. Many projects in engineering will not need one but most projects in science will.

If you do have a hypothesis then part of your project will be to test its validity and so show either that it cannot be supported and that some other statement is more appropriate or that it can be supported. A hypothesis may be tested by logical argument based on evidence (with or without field data) or, more likely in science and engineering, by statistical analysis.

If it is to be tested by logical argument the process is sometime known as the dialectic of research. This involves testing the ideas using reason and logic and the process is often called Hegel's critical method, after the German 'idealistic' philosopher Georg Wilhelm Friedrich Hegel (1770–1831).

In this method an unsubstantiated statement, the hypothesis, is made and arguments in support of it (the thesis) and against it (the antithesis) are put forward. These arguments are examined and weighed and from consideration of them the truth of the

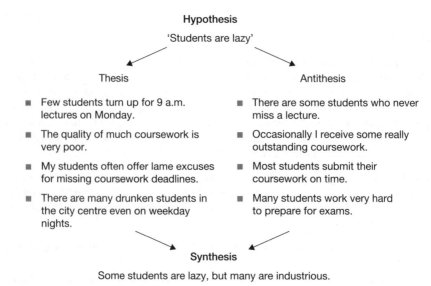

Figure 2.1 Logical argument

matter (the synthesis) emerges. Here, in Figure 2.1, is an example. Let's be provocative and suppose that I, as a lecturer, put forward the hypothesis that 'students are lazy' . . .

You can probably put forward many more arguments for and against the hypothesis. If they are all for, or all against, then you might examine how objective and unbiased you are.

At this stage it would be possible to test the validity of the synthesis by taking it as a new hypothesis, find arguments in support of and against the new hypothesis and so refine the synthesis. If the synthesis is valid there will be few, if any, arguments against it.

The alternative is to test the hypothesis by statistical methods. For example, if the aim of the project was 'to investigate how the rate of accidents affects the profitability of a company' then you might put forward the hypothesis that:

Null hypothesis

The rate of accidents has no effect upon the profitability of a company.

This is called the 'null hypothesis' and it is this that you seek to support or otherwise. To do this you also need an 'alternative hypothesis' such as:

Alternative hypothesis

A high accident rate has a negative effect upon the profitability of a company.

You need to show either that the null hypothesis is true at a given level of confidence, or that it is not true and therefore the alternative hypothesis is true, at the same level of confidence.

In this example it would appear that there is a third alternative, that 'a high accident rate has a *positive* effect upon the profitability of a company'. Fortunately this flies in the face of reason since, if true, it would mean that it would be in a company's best interest to make you, as an employee, have an accident. If that were really the case you should find another job!

'Key questions' are those rather specific questions that you might need to get answers to, in order to achieve your objectives. If you have any of these, they should be listed separately. You will need to ensure that they are all addressed within your methodology.

2.9 Resources

Now you know what it is that you want to investigate, it is important that you have the wherewithal to do so. This is the last part of the planning process and having got to this stage you will probably have spotted whether there are any key physical resources that you do not have access to. However, the need for financial, electronic, data and human resources may be less obvious. Do not make any assumptions about their availability at this stage. If something is critical to your project and you later discover that you do not have it, you could be in trouble.

The physical resources include the technology you are investigating and the technology you are investigating it with. Do not forget all the clips, cables, batteries, electronic media and attachments that go with both. Identify where they are all to come from and make sure you have them.

> **Confirm with your institution that it is willing and able to provide the resources you would like it to provide.**

Consider your liability for anything borrowed and the need for insurance. A digital camera will be useful for recording your work. Will you need transport and if so what will it be and can you afford it? Testing your ideas might be delightful in Delhi but cheaper in Chester.

If there are any financial implications regarding the conduct of your project then prepare a list and find the cost of the items. If anything is very expensive, will a cheaper alternative do, or can you do without it altogether? Do not forget the service items like fuel for a vehicle or mobile phone costs if you need contact with a colleague while collecting data at remote sites.

Your electronic resources include any computing hardware and software that you need. You should have easy access to computers at your institution but do you also need a laptop or data logger in the laboratory or in the field? Do you have any specialist software that you need and is it installed on your computer? Do you have the necessary passwords, authorisation codes, files or dongles and will they continue to be valid throughout your investigation? Make sure you know how to use your software. Again, make sure that you have all your electronic resources and do not make any assumptions about their availability.

If you intend to use any data sets gathered by others, i.e. secondary data, then identify what they are and confirm that you have access to them. Check to see if there are any restrictions on their use such as those of copyright, confidentiality or accessibility. Is a cost involved? If you intend to rely on data from questionnaires or interviews, consider all the issues covered in Chapter 3. You must ensure that you will get the data you need and consider alternatives in case things go wrong.

The most important human resource is you.

Do you have the time to undertake the whole of your proposed project, bearing in mind that you probably have other academic work to complete at the same time?

Is there a risk element to your project? There probably will be if you are doing any laboratory work or fieldwork. Your institution will almost certainly require you to do a risk assessment and this should highlight any unacceptable risks that will need to be reviewed. Do this openly and honestly. It is in your best interests that you do not risk injury to yourself or others and you might invalidate any insurance if you do not complete a full risk assessment. The issues of health, safety and risk assessments and the Control of Substances Hazardous to Health regulations are covered in Chapter 3.

Likewise, you will need to consider the ethical issues associated with your project. Although you might think there are none, depending on what you intend to do, you will probably be required to complete an ethical assessment for your project. Again, there are more details in Chapter 3.

For the GPS-bike project your resources list might look like this:

Resources

Physical resources
I will provide

    Homemade attachment to attach GPS receiver to bike

    Car with roof rack to transport bike to site

    Mountain bike

Need to confirm

    Access to mountain bike race circuit

University will provide

    GPS receiver including cables and batteries

    Biometric sensors

Financial resources

    Transport fuel costs

    Insurance

Electronic resources

    Laptop

GPS download software

Biometric software

Processing software (Excel)

Data resources

Ordnance Survey's GPS Active Network data

Human resources

I am the bike rider and data gatherer

A friend to assist during data collection and for safety

The resources for the physics project are much simpler in that all the facilities and consumables will be found in the laboratory. It is therefore simply necessary to identify what they are and either to confirm that they are available, or make sure that they can and will be obtained in good time.

2.10 Timetable

You will have been given what seems to be an extraordinary amount of time to complete your project and dissertation. Do not be fooled. This is not just your tutor's idea of how to get the coursework setting out of the way at the beginning of the year. Completing the project/dissertation is a big job and will take the time that has been allocated to it.

You will have deadlines to meet so it is essential to have a plan. If you have a whole year to complete your project it may seem like forever, at the beginning. As you work from one deadline to the next deadline in all the other work you have to do, it is tempting to put off the project work. It will be fatal if you do; there is too much to do to let it all drift by.

A timetabled plan is essential.

By having a plan you will be able to monitor your progress and hopefully will be able to take comfort in seeing that your work is on, or even ahead of, schedule. More likely it will be the other way around, in which case you will get an early warning that you need to put in more effort. A plan is just a baseline for action and as your project progresses you may need to modify the plan or even develop a new one.

Your timetable might be in the form of a bar chart or a series of timed milestones. The bar chart would look something like Figure 2.2, but usually with more detail that is specific to your project than it is possible to show here.

In this table there are the three deadlines: submitting the project proposal; submitting the dissertation; and attending the viva voce. There are a number of activities that need to be completed before each deadline. Some of the activities depend upon previous activities being started if not completed.

Make sure that if there are periods when you will unable to work on the project they are shown. You may be away for a week at a time on a holiday, expedition, trip abroad, wedding (especially if it's your own) or field course. Each of these may not amount to

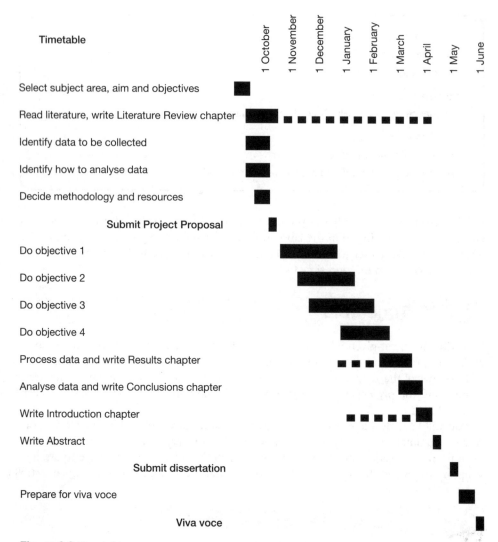

Figure 2.2 Timetable

much but added together would take a month out of your programme. If you need to set aside time for revision just before an exam, take that out also. Many things can go wrong, so although you may not add much slack into the written timetable be prepared to put in the extra time when your computer crashes and you forgot to create backup files.

Notice that there is a gap of about two weeks between 'Write Abstract' and 'Submit Dissertation'. That is not just there as a safety net but will probably be needed for you to get the dissertation printed and bound. Remember that everybody else will be doing just the same thing at the same time. Murphy's Law states that if things can go wrong, they will. Murphy's Second Law is that if they are going to go wrong, they will do so at the last possible moment.

Time allocation calculation

Date now   17 October

Final hand-in date   14 May

Hence   30 weeks available

Less   2 weeks each for Christmas and Easter
       1 week each for course field trip, exams and end of term
       (×2) coursework deadlines, holiday with girl/boy friend,
       contingencies

Hence   20 weeks available in practice

Hours allocated to the module (will depend on the module's size)

                                  300

Therefore time I must spend each week on the project *because I want the project to be manageable and I intend to do well!*

$$= {}^{300}/_{20} = 15 \text{ hours}$$

Figure 2.3 Time allocation calculation

Even with such a simple bar chart as Figure 2.2 it is likely that you will have difficulty making all the activities fit. If nothing else it will make you realise that you may not have all the time you thought you had and so will have to make some compromises to fit all the stages in.

You will need to calculate the time you need to allocate to working on the project. There is a simple calculation in Figure 2.3. Of course, this will only work if you use the allocated time efficiently and productively.

2.11 Example project proposal

Box 2.1 shows an example of an MSc project proposal.

Box 2.1 An MSc project proposal

Acceptance envelope and permeability testing of Compacted Clay Liners
Paul Rushton
Rationale: Landfill sites are designed to entomb waste mass from the surrounding environment. This 'encapsulation system' generally comprises a 'basal and sidewall liner' and following the cessation of waste deposition a 'top liner' commonly referred to as a cap. The most common types of lining material are naturally occurring cohesive materials.

These materials are then processed, and tested with the primary objective of achieving the required hydraulic conductivity necessary to prevent an unacceptable discharge of leachate and landfill gas from the landfill into the surrounding groundwater and strata (Gallagher et al., 2003).

The earliest Compacted Clay Liners (CCL) were formed using specifications developed from structural fill civil engineering projects (Daniel, 1990) where the main criterion was to achieve adequate strength and compressibility necessary for highway works. These general specifications have since been adapted and refined to achieve the required hydraulic conductivity. Historically the standard specification for a clay liner was primarily to achieve a hydraulic conductivity (commonly termed as permeability) no greater than 1×10^{-9} m/s at a thickness of 1 m. This standard is achievable with many naturally occurring clays within the UK and this requirement has been assessed as the main criterion in order to restrict the discharge of pollutants (gas and leachate) through the liner into the surrounding environment to an acceptable level. Another key requirement of a CCL is that it must have 'as good a plastic deformability as possible and sufficient strength' (Holzlohner, 1995) in order to ensure that the liner lasts the lifetime design period.

In order to achieve the necessary permeability, strength and durability the placement criteria for a CCL are normally defined by specific geotechnical index tests and thus an 'Acceptance Envelope' (AE) is derived. The AE comprises a Lower Moisture Content (LMC) value, an Upper Moisture Content (UMC) value and an allowable air voids content. When defining the LMC the optimum moisture content, or plastic limit, or 5% air voids should be used, whichever is the higher (Department of the Environment, 1996). The criteria used to define the UMC are dictated by the shear strength of the clay. In general it is accepted within the construction industry that a minimum shear strength of 50 Kpa is essential to support plant trafficability and enable compaction. Consideration should also be given to the shear strength value used in the CCL stability risk assessment (Environment Agency, 2003a). Typically values used in such assessments often range between 50 and 70 Kpa.

It is essential therefore that the permeability testing undertaken is accurate and representative of the 'actual' in-situ permeability. In England permeability testing has predominantly been undertaken in accordance with the 'British Standard constant head triaxial test' (BS1377:1990, Part 6, Method 6). Following the publication of the Environment Agency's R and D report in 2003 (Environment Agency, 2003b) the use of the Accelerated Permeability (AP) test has since become fairly widespread. The author's experience of both permeability test methods is that the occurrence of a permeability value less than the required regulatory standard is extremely rare. Given the fairly high material variability in many CCL and also human error this is somewhat surprising and needs further investigation.

Various studies undertaken in the USA have found that permeability measured in the field (K_f) can be between 10 to 1000 times higher than the measured laboratory permeability (K_l) value (Daniel, 1984; Elsbury et al., 1990). Further work from the USA has also shown that approximately 26% of CCL landfill data reviewed showed that the K_f failed to meet the appropriate minimum permeability requirement of $<1 \times 10^{-9}$ m/s (Benson et al., 1999) despite the K_l values at the time of the liner construction being satisfactory.

Technical officers from the Midlands Region of the Environment Agency (EA) are frequently told by waste management companies/consultancies that the criteria used to derive the AE are inconsistent compared to those being applied in other areas of the EA. For certain materials within the Midlands Region, such as the Mercia Mudstone and

Etruria Marl formations, these envelopes are often so small that the clay resource is not considered suitable.

It may be that the EA is therefore placing unreasonable constraints on the use of some clays. The EA may be condemning clay reserves as being unsuitable when in fact they are not. It is therefore critical that research is undertaken to establish how the correct AE is derived in order for the EA to adopt a consistent approach. Additionally it is important to assess how consistently within the waste management industry these constraints are being applied.

Aim: The aim of the project is to investigate placement criteria of CCL used in the construction of low permeability landfill liners including the validity of the permeability testing undertaken.

Objectives:

1. To investigate how an acceptance envelope should be derived correctly.
2. To determine how consistently CCL acceptance envelopes have been derived in the past.
3. To investigate the relationship between K_f and K_l.
4. To estimate the number of previously constructed CCL liners which may have permeability below the required value.

Key questions:

1. How consistent has the derivation of CCL acceptance envelopes been?
2. What is the relationship between K_f and K_l for CCL in England?
3. How should CCL acceptance envelopes be derived?

Outline methodology:

Stage 1: Literature review   Examine the relevant literature available on the issue of the correct derivation of an acceptance envelope for a CCL. Particular attention will be given to permeability testing and the relative shortcomings of the methods used. Textbooks, regulatory guidance documentation, technical/scientific journals, seminar/conference proceedings and research papers will be consulted.

Stage 2: Collating and analysing the data   Review and analyse published CCL data contained within Construction Quality Assurance reports available on the public register. This will be undertaken for a large number of landfill sites across the country in order for the study to be representative of the eight regional areas regulated by the EA. This information is available from the EA's electronic data management system at all EA offices.

Stage 3: Fieldwork   Measure the K_f and K_l values and find correlation values. The correlation will then be used together with the findings and theoretical framework contained within Benson (1999) to achieve objective 4.

Proposed structure: Chapters:

1. Background to the problem
2. Review of acceptance envelope procedures
3. Review of permeability testing
4. Data collection and analysis results and table compilation

5. Field study and presentation of results

6. Analysis of fieldwork

7. Discussion and critical appraisal

8. Conclusions and recommendations for further research

References

Initial references:

Benson, C.H., Daniel, D.E., and Boutwell, G.P. (1999). Field performance of compacted clay liners. Journal of geotechnical and geoenvironmental engineering, May 1999, pp 390–403.

Daniel, D.E. (1984). Predicting hydraulic conductivity of clay liners. Journal of geotechnical engineering, volume 110 (No. 2), pp 285–300.

Daniel, D.E., Benson, C.H. (1990). Water content-density criteria for compacted soil liners. Journal of geotechnical engineering, volume 116 (No. 12), pp 1811–1830.

Department of the Environment (1996). Guidance on good practice for landfill engineering Report No.CWM 106/94c. Abingdon: Waste management information bureau.

Elsbury, B.R., et al. (1990). Field and laboratory testing of a compacted soil liner: EPA project summary. Cincinnati, Ohio: United States Environmental Protection Agency, EPA/600/S2-88/067. Jan 1990, pp 1–7.

Environment Agency (2003a). Stability of landfill lining systems: report numbers 1 and 2, R & D technical report P1-385/TR1. Bristol: Environment Agency.

Environment Agency (2003b). Procedure for the determination of the permeability of clayey soils in a triaxial cell using the accelerated permeability test – R & D technical report P1-398/TR/1. Bristol: Environment Agency.

Gallagher, E.M.G., Needham, A., and Smith, D.M. (2003). Use of geosynthetics in landfill steepwall lining systems. In: Dixon, et al., ed. Geosynthetics: protecting the environment, Proceedings of the 1st IGS UK chapter National Geosynthetics Symposium, Nottingham Trent University, 17 June 2003. London: Thomas Telford, pp 71–91.

Holzlohner, U., et al. (1995), Landfill liner systems. Sunderland: Penshaw Press.

Resources required: In order to collect, process and analyse the data, access to appropriate computer software packages is essential; this is available on the author's employer's computer network.

The K_f testing will be funded by a number of waste management companies/environmental consultancies as a research project whilst running in tandem with CCL construction projects. The management and coordination of the field testing will be undertaken by the author; this will include regular site visits to ensure that the works are being undertaken in accordance with the specification.

In order to manage the above fieldwork in a safe manner the author will need to ensure that the necessary Personal Protective Equipment (PPE) is worn at all times and the Dynamic Risk Assessment for the site and activities being undertaken is thoroughly read and complied with.

Anticipated outcomes: Discovery of what assessment criteria have been previously used in the determination of CCL acceptance envelopes.

Clarification of the relationship between permeability testing undertaken in the laboratory compared to in-situ permeability testing for CCL constructed in England.

Find the best method to establish the acceptance envelope of a CCL.

Programme of work: not shown here

Now you have done most of the preliminary planning and are ready to complete your own project proposal. Good luck, and enjoy!

2.12 Summary

- Select your project by identifying what interests you and then narrowing the subject down until it is very well focused.
- Rephrase your question as your aim.
- Identify the three to five objectives that need to be satisfied to fulfil your aim.
- If you use case studies they should be used to produce examples, not be the dissertation itself.
- Beware of using only one or two case studies. You may have very little to 'compare and contrast'.
- Think through your methodology in detail. Do not assume you will be able to fill in the blanks later.
- If you have a hypothesis, how will you test it? By logic and reason or by statistical methods?
- Identify all the physical, financial, electronic, data and human resources you are going to need and where they are going to come from.
- Prepare a timetabled plan of action and stick to it. If you cannot, then revise your plan. Make sure that it is realistic, not just possible. Allow time for delays and foul-ups; they will happen.

What next?

Get started now!

Find a subject you enjoy.

Think of a question.

Rephrase as the aim.

Identify the objectives.

Decide how you are going to do the work; your methodology.

Work out how you are going to analyse the data.

List the resources and make sure you will have them all.

Write your project proposal – follow your institution's guidance and this chapter.

Get your tutor or a trusted friend to review your project proposal and make suggestions.

Do the risk and ethical assessments.

Submit your project proposal on time!

CHAPTER

3

Hard work or pleasure?

3.1 Getting stuck in

So you got the project proposal in on time, but only just.

But well done anyway. Now you have to get on with the job and at this stage that is about fulfilling those objectives by applying your chosen methodology. Hopefully you did at least skim through this chapter and decided on the nature of the data you were going to collect and how you would process it. Further in this chapter we will consider the classifications of the broad ways of collecting data you could use and the implications of these methods. So, here are some issues you will need to consider and more ideas for your methodology.

The aim of this chapter is to make you aware of the issues that you will have to consider in the conduct of your project and to be able to collect qualitative data. By the end of this chapter you should be able to:

- **Understand the importance of health and safety.**
- **Understand the broad categories of data collection methods.**
- **Construct a questionnaire.**
- **Conduct interviews.**

3.2 The science and engineering context

When you do research as an engineer or scientist there are some factors that make the enterprise different from research in other disciplines such as in the arts and the humanities. Typically science and engineering research involves experimental design, measurement and numerical data processing leading to results, often statistical, drawn from data processing. The meaning or interpretation of those results is part of the analysis.

Such an approach is said to be *quantitative*. Alternatively research may be *qualitative* and so be concerned with experience, description or opinion and meaning derived from analysis of data found from investigating these phenomena. The use of qualitative data is less usual in science and engineering but by no means unheard of; it all depends on what you are investigating as to which is the most appropriate method.

● 3.3 Health, safety and risk assessment

Your institution will be most concerned to make sure of your health and safety while you are studying with it. It is not just that your tutors are kind and caring, which they probably are, but because the law sets certain standards and creates duties of care. Therefore it is most likely that your institution will require you to complete a risk assessment before you start any fieldwork or use a laboratory. The object of the exercise is to remove any unacceptable level of risk that you might expose yourself or others to. Also, your institution needs to protect itself from any legal liability for your actions.

> **The risk assessment should identify the risks concerned and evaluate their potential for harm.**

If, as a result, the risk or the potential harm is too great then it will be necessary either to put measures in place to reduce the risk or harm, or to find alternative activities to the ones proposed.

A risk assessment is something we are all familiar with. Every day you make a risk assessment when you cross the road. You are probably not conscious of doing so; it has become second nature. What you are doing is assessing the likelihood of harm and the severity of that harm should it occur. If traffic is moving slowly in an urban environment the risk of being struck may be more than remote but the consequence if you were could be little more than bruising or a broken bone at worst. On the other hand, if you were about to cross a fast highway you would make sure that there was virtually no chance of being struck by a car as the outcome would almost certainly be death.

To assess risk you will first need to identify all the hazards associated with your project. Next decide who could be harmed and how that harm could occur. Evaluate the risks and identify the appropriate precautions to take. Make a record of your conclusions and ensure that you carry out the precautions you have identified. At appropriate intervals review your assessment and update it if necessary.

One way of evaluating risk is to use two sets of numbers. One describes the likelihood of a hazard from, say, 1 = remote possibility to 5 = almost certain. Another range of numbers describes the severity of the hazard should it occur, from, say, 1 = minor cuts or bruises to 5 = death. Then take the product of the two numbers.

Example

If there is a remote possibility of death

the product would be $1 \times 5 = 5$.

If there are almost certain to be minor cuts or bruises

the product would be $5 \times 1 = 5$.

At the extreme ends of the range would be the remote possibility of minor cuts or bruises ($1 \times 1 = 1$) and almost certain death ($5 \times 5 = 25$). Whereas the former risk might be acceptable, the latter most certainly would not.

It would be unwise to make a decision on the acceptability of the risk based only on the numbers and their product alone. However, if the product is much above 1 then you should consider what remedial steps to take to reduce the risk and if the risk cannot be brought down, then the proposed activity will have to be abandoned.

> **No matter how good you think your project is, the health, safety and indeed life of yourself and others come first.**

Your institution will have its own risk evaluation form and procedures. You should follow them exactly. If any of the advice here conflicts with the guidance from your institution, follow your institution's instructions. If you are at all uncertain about how to do the risk assessment, seek the advice of your tutors. Do not be tempted to underplay the risk to avoid having to modify your project.

A useful leaflet from the UK's Health and Safety Executive (HSE) may be found at http://www.hse.gov.uk/pubns/indg163.pdf.

● 3.4 COSHH

The Control of Substances Hazardous to Health or COSHH regulations of the HSE govern the use of a number of hazardous substances. The COSHH regulations require that a series of eight measures are undertaken. They are to:

■ gauge risks;
■ select precautions;
■ stop or manage the exposure;
■ put control measures in place;
■ observe the exposure;
■ monitor health of subjects;
■ plan for accidents and emergencies;
■ ensure proper training and supervision.

There is a substantial website at http://www.hse.gov.uk/coshh where there is specific guidance in the form of free leaflets, on working with a variety of chemicals and metals, biological agents and biological monitoring, and personal protective equipment.

If you expect to be working with any hazardous substances you should first consult with your tutor who will probably take advice from your institution's health and safety officer.

For each substance that you intend to work with, it will be necessary to identify how that substance will be used and the hazard that may be created by its use. For example, working with wet sand is unlikely to cause a great hazard on its own but if dry sand is used in a grinding process then there will be a significant hazard from airborne silica particles.

Substances need to be assessed in isolation and in combination. Two substances which are stable on their own may be much more hazardous in combination. For example, household bleach and ammonia are reasonably safe when separate but mixed together produce chloramine fumes.

Just as with health and safety in the last section, the risk and severity of the hazard must be assessed and appropriate control measures put in place. If the risk and severity cannot be reduced to an acceptable level then that part of the project will have to be abandoned.

> **It is essential to seek competent advice before undertaking the risk assessment.**

You will need to consult with your tutor and the responsible person in your laboratory. There will be procedures that you must adhere to; the more potentially dangerous the substance the more exhaustive the procedures. Special regulations will apply where radiological or biohazards are present.

Box 3.1 shows an abbreviated risk assessment for a laboratory experiment on the measurement of liquid crystal switching.

Box 3.1 An abbreviated risk assessment

Hazards	Control measures (see key below)	People at risk	Risk	Action
Injury from handling heavy equipment	Follow institution policy on manual handling (S P F)	Operators (institution students and staff), maintenance personnel	N/A	Apply policy
Harmful and toxic materials	Follow institution policy. Perform COSHH assessments on materials (S P F)		N/A	Apply policy
Shock hazard, mains electricity	Follow institution policy on electrical safety (S P F)		N/A	Apply policy
Eyestrain, strain due to bad posture: display screen equipment	Follow institution policy. Display screen assessment may be necessary (S P F)		N/A	Apply policy
General	Make users aware of emergency exit and nearest first aider (G U)		N/A	N/A

Hazards	Control measures (see key below)	People at risk	Risk	Action
Hazard to heart pacemakers from magnetic fields (up to 1 Tesla)	Containment: Put magnet against a wall. Warning (N): Equipment in inner darkroom, sign on outside of room which has only one entry point		HIGH: likely to cause loss of life (major severity) possible when activity takes place (medium frequency)	Risk reduction requiring urgent action: check field leakage into corridor, check field safety levels for pacemakers
Eye damage from laser radiation having wavelength 633 nm, intensity < 5 mW, class 3a red He-Ne	Protection: Use laser safety goggles (PPE). Warning and Containment: sign outside room (N). Instructions given to users (T F)		VERY HIGH: loss of sight injury (major severity) possible each time activity takes place (high frequency)	Risk reduction – urgent: check radiation levels compared with eye/skin max exposure levels
Physical injury hazard from falling equipment or from strain by moving heavy equipment	Make arrangement as sturdy as possible. Follow Institution Safety Policy on Manual Handling (S)		HIGH: dislocation /fracture injury (major severity) possible a few times when activity takes place (medium frequency)	Risk reduction requiring urgent action: review controls, e.g. use of clamps and fixings
High currents from electromagnet power supply	Containment (F): terminals from power supply are shielded – cannot be accidentally accessed as they are between the power supply and the wall		MEDIUM: risk of death by electrocution (major severity) just feasible (low likelihood)	Consider risk reduction: review controls and security of enclosure

A   Authorised staff only
C   COSHH assessment
S   Institution Safety Policy
F   Manufacturer's guidelines
G   Good Housekeeping
I   Isolation devices; Trips
M   Assessment required
N   Notices; Information
P   Standard Operating Procedures

PPE Personal Protective Equipment
T   Training required
V   Local Exhaust Ventilation
X   Guards; Barriers
Assessed by......
Date.................

3.5 Ethics

Ethics is concerned with 'right' and 'wrong'. Your project should be conducted in an ethical way so that what you do is right and so that you do no wrong to any person, animal or the environment. The Economic and Social Research Council (ERSC) identifies six key principles for ethical research, so you should:

- carry out your investigation to ensure integrity and quality;
- inform your assistants and subjects about the reason for, methods and possible applications of your work;
- respect confidentiality and anonymity of those involved;
- not apply pressure on others to take part;
- not cause harm;
- ensure your research is independent and unbiased by conflict of interest.

> **If your intended work looks as if it might contradict any of these principles, discuss it with your tutor first.**

If you intend any experimental work with living vertebrate animals it will be subject to the Animals (Scientific Procedures) Act 1986. Some institutions would not allow this for an undergraduate research project. If you use human volunteers as experimental subjects, for example using human tissue samples, observing physiological or biochemical response to exercise, conducting psychometric tests or exposing subjects to higher doses of chemicals, magnetic/electrical fields or radiation than they would receive in everyday life then you will almost certainly need ethical approval.

You will need to take particular care if your research may involve vulnerable people such as children, pregnant women, prisoners, those over 65 years of age or those with mental illness. If you do intend to involve vulnerable persons they should be chaperoned by someone of the same sex who is not the investigator. Be particularly careful if you intend to investigate sensitive issues such as those involving other people's political views or possible criminal activity.

You should avoid having to take bodily samples or any activity that is likely to cause distress whether emotional or physical. You should not expose your participants to any distress or hazard beyond that met in everyday life. If you intend to observe or record your participants' behaviour they need to be informed beforehand.

Your participants must give informed consent, so they must be told of the objectives of your investigation and what will happen to the data that are collected. If children or those with mental illness are to be involved then the consent must be obtained from a responsible person such as a parent or guardian.

All participants must be informed that they have the right to withdraw from the investigation at any time and require that any data collected that relates to them will be destroyed.

All participants should be asked to review and sign a consent form. The contents of the form will vary with the research. The form below may be adapted to suit the purpose of your research. You may need to add other paragraphs.

Consent form for interview on . . . *subject of interview* . . .

Purpose of research
I understand that the purpose of this research is to . . . *reason for research* . . .

Extent of my permission
I give permission for this interview to be recorded by audio/video and for the interview to be transcribed. These data may only be used by . . . *name of researcher* . . . of . . . *name of institution* . . . I understand that one outcome of this research will be a written dissertation or journal paper which may enter the public domain.

My right to comment
I am informed that I will receive a copy of the transcribed interview so I may review and make comment. I will be given . . . *number* . . . working days during which I may withdraw the information before it is included in the dissertation or other work.

Limitation of anonymity
I understand that as the research is specific and the number of interviewees is small, complete anonymity cannot be assured and that anonymous quotations may be used.

My questions
I have read this form and have had any part I do not understand explained to my satisfaction.

Confidentiality
I understand that . . . *name of researcher* . . . will treat all data I provide in a confidential manner. The data will be recorded so that I may not be recognised unless I give permission for my identity to be revealed.

My permission
I **DO NOT / DO** give permission for the information I have given, whether as direct quotes and/or in paraphrased form, to be linked to my name.

My right to stop
I understand that I participate in this interview voluntarily and consent to taking part on the strict understanding that I can withdraw at any time without having to explain why.

_____   _____   _____
Name of participant   Signature of participant   Date

_____   _____
Name of interviewer   Signature of interviewer

The consent form must be clear and unambiguous and you should design it for a reader with less than average intelligence for your target group or with dyslexia, to ensure that all will understand it easily. Do not use a small type font, 12-point minimum, and only justify to the left-hand margin. Keep sentences and paragraphs short. Lay the form out with headings and/or bullet points. Avoid technical terms in the text and use the active voice. Undertake a pilot test to assess how other people comprehend the form.

Check the readability of your text by using the option in Microsoft Word. Readability statistics are displayed when you have completed 'Spelling and Grammar' on the 'Tools' menu. On the 'Tools' menu you must first click 'Options', and then click the

'Spelling & Grammar' tab. Then check the 'Check grammar with spelling' and 'Show readability statistics' check boxes.

The Data Protection Act 1998 will have to be complied with, particularly as regards the storage of data. Audio and video data should be kept in a safe place and not given to a third party. Such data should be destroyed when no longer required for the investigation.

There are particular issues associated with secondary data. If you are using data from other sources then you will need to make sure that your use of the data will not conflict with any of the principles above. Likewise, you should consider how others may make use of any data that you make available.

Be cautious of making a confidentiality agreement in exchange for being given commercially sensitive information. Check with your tutor to see if your dissertation will be made publicly available. If your tutor submits your dissertation to a web-based plagiarism detection service then it effectively goes into the public domain. Your institution may not allow you to submit a dissertation with confidential information in it. If your institution has a code of practice for ethical research, which it probably does, you should consult it.

> **The fundamental principle is that you must do no harm.**

If your research is being sponsored then it is likely that ethical monitoring will be required if the project involves research on humans and animals.

If you intend to use people, human tissue, or tissue of recently deceased persons, or animals whether wild or captive, then your project must have a serious research purpose if it is to meet ethical standards. Your institution will have an approval process that identifies such projects that need ethical review. There will probably be a standard checklist for making that assessment. You will not be permitted to start a project of this nature without formal approval from the appropriate ethics committee. If your project involves the National Health Service or social care issues the ethical review will be undertaken outside your institution. Here are two sample checklists for identifying investigations that will need ethical approval.

If you answer **YES** to any of these questions ethical approval will be required.

Will you undertake physically invasive procedures?

Will you be taking bodily samples?

Will your participants be under 18, over 65, pregnant women, people with mental illness, detained persons or other vulnerable groups?

Will you undertake home visits?

Might you cause physical or psychological distress?

Will your participants be challenged physically or psychologically, e.g. will there be physical exercise or financial risk?

Will your participants be exposed to risks or distress greater than those found in everyday life?

Will you use hazardous materials?

Are you in direct authority over your participants, e.g. as a sports coach training young athletes?

Have you been offered incentives (e.g. sponsorship) to conduct the investigation?

Will you be offering incentives to your participants?

If you answer **NO** to any of these questions ethical approval will be required.

Have you been trained in the methods you intend to use?

Will vulnerable persons be chaperoned by two or more investigators at all times?

Will there be an investigator of the same sex as the participant(s) present at all times?

Will you inform participants that you intend to observe or record them?

Will your participants give informed consent freely?

Will you tell your participants of the investigation's objectives and how the data are to be used?

Will consent be obtained from a responsible person where children under 18 or particip-ants with impaired understanding or communication are involved?

Will you tell your participants that they can withdraw at any time without having to give reasons and that they can require that data about them or gathered from them to be destroyed?

Will your participants give informed consent freely, including those who may be under pressure to take part such as persons in the armed forces, employees or students?

If you use deception will you tell your participants of the true objectives of your invest-igation at the earliest possible opportunity?

Have you considered how deceived participants may react to the truth of the investigation?

Will you keep all personal data confidential and anonymous unless it has been agreed in advance or is required by law?

Will you comply with the Data Protection Act 1998?

Will you keep video or audio recordings of participants in a secure place and not release them to third parties?

Will you destroy such recordings on completing the investigation?

If you are working with animals then special considerations will apply. For example, if you are working with horses or other farm animals then it is likely that you will be required to ensure that the 'five freedoms' as defined by the Farm Animal Welfare Council are respected. These may be found at http://www.fawc.org.uk/freedoms.htm but can be summarised as freedom:

1. from hunger and thirst – access to fresh water and suitable food;

2. from discomfort – right environment with shelter and rest;

3. from pain, injury or disease – by prevention, diagnosis and treatment;

4. to express normal behaviour – with space, facilities and the company of the same kind of animal;

5. from fear and distress – conditions and treatment to avoid mental suffering.

Your institution's research ethics committee will need to be assured that:

■ your project does not risk harm to the person, emotion or reputation of the participants, including yourself, and the committee will want to know of the steps you will take to prevent harm;

■ you have suitable arrangements for recruiting participants and getting their informed consent; copies of information sheets and consent forms will be required;

■ you can justify the need for any surveillance methods that are not obvious to your participants;

■ you can keep any personal data secure and confidential and anonymous;

■ you are using the minimum number of participants required to satisfy your research goals;

■ you have suitable arrangements for keeping personal data or tissue and for their disposal when the project is finished;

■ you will debrief your participants;

■ you have had the necessary Criminal Records Bureau checks if you intend to work with children or vulnerable adults;

■ you have the necessary consent from the patient or from the deceased's relatives if you intend to use a deceased's bodily materials;

■ you will obtain a Home Office licence before starting work if you intend to use animals under the Animals (Scientific Procedures) Act 1986. Details are on the Home Office website at http://scienceandresearch.homeoffice.gov.uk/animal-research/. If your project involves working with animals then your institution will have strict procedures that you will need to follow.

If the committee declines to authorise your project you should be given feedback so that it may be possible to revise the project to make it acceptable.

You may be thinking that there is a lot of bureaucracy here and that you would rather just keep quiet and get on with the project and hope that nobody will notice. Inevitably, when your tutors read your dissertation your lack of ethical approval will become obvious and you face the serious risks of failing the project and institutional disciplinary action. You should include a statement in your dissertation stating how the ethical approval was obtained and how you kept to its terms.

In conducting your project you may find yourself facing a conflict of interest; that is, a conflict between your own interests and your responsibility to act ethically. It will be your responsibility to manage that conflict and if you do not do so you risk failing the project or disciplinary action. If there is great pressure on you to succeed in your project and you will gain much by doing so then there may be a temptation to act unethically. If this is the case, resist the temptation. If you do find yourself tempted to act unethically, discuss the situation with your tutor who may be able to help you find a way around the problem. Consider where your project is placed by referring to Figure 3.1.

If things are not going well in your project you may find that you are tempted to make up (fabricate) data or change (falsify) your data to fit the conclusions that you

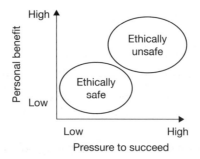

Figure 3.1 The temptation to act unethically

would like to draw. If you are caught doing so then the penalties are likely to be severe because these are forms of cheating. If your research is funded then you damage your institution's reputation as well as your own and funding may not be forthcoming for others in the future.

By understanding the nature of possible misconduct in research you will be in a position to avoid some common errors. If you were to use other people's ideas without proper acknowledgement, that would be piracy. Similarly, using other people's text without proper acknowledgement would be plagiarism. There is a whole chapter (Chapter 8) on this all too common academic crime. Misrepresentation is where you try to present facts or the ideas of others in a false or unfair way. Fraud is deliberate deception, including fabricating or falsifying data. Acting recklessly is where you create risk or harm to people, animals or the environment by not following established procedures.

However, if you make an honest error or your research is just of poor quality and you had no intention to deceive then you would probably not be guilty of misconduct.

Not everything requires ethical approval. If the data you are after are publicly and lawfully available, for example in libraries or as statistics published by government departments, you need take no further action.

There is further useful information on the subject of ethics from the Economic and Social Research Council at http://www.esrc.ac.uk/ESRCInfoCentre/Images/ESRC_ Re_Ethics_Frame_tcm6-11291.pdf.

● 3.6 Proving your point

Your project aims to find out something by answering a question. But can you ever be sure that you have found the one and only true answer? In other words, is it ever possible to prove that something is so? Even proof has its shades of grey. Consider these phrases:

On the balance of probabilities
Beyond a reasonable doubt
Beyond a shadow of a doubt
With absolute certainty

Clearly these statements are in increasing order of confidence of the issue in question. However, only the first and last can have any numerical values put on them. The balance of probabilities implies that something is as likely to be true as it is not, i.e. in numerical terms it is 0.5 or 50%. Absolute certainty implies confidence in the truth at the level of 1.0 or 100%. 'On the balance of probabilities' is unlikely to be of any great interest; it is almost the equivalent of saying 'I just don't know'. Seldom if ever can you be 100% certain about a fact that has been deduced when dealing with experiments or fieldwork. The two in the middle have legal connotations but no legal definition. The law and statistics are uneasy bedfellows.

If you undertake experiments or fieldwork you are likely to come to conclusions which have calculable uncertainty. From this you will be able to state the confidence levels associated with your results. So whatever your outcomes you will almost invariably be able to come to conclusions. It is comforting to know that you can expect to produce valid conclusions, even if the results seem less than you might wish them to be.

● 3.7 Quantitative or qualitative methods

In research one generally adopts either 'qualitative' or 'quantitative' methods. As the names suggest, quantitative methods are concerned with numbers and qualitative methods are not. Generally speaking, engineers and scientists more usually employ quantitative rather than qualitative methods, but that is something of a broad generalisation so it is appropriate to consider both.

3.7.1 Quantitative methods

Quantitative research, as the name implies, is concerned with investigating problems which can be represented in terms of numbers. Mathematical modelling may be used. To obtain the numbers it is usual to make measurements, which in turn are used to derive mathematical expressions for relationships between the various phenomena under investigation.

For example, if you want to investigate how a particular wood that might be used as a building material behaves, then you might devise experiments to discover how beams made from the wood bend or permanently deform under different loadings and in turn under different conditions of temperature and moisture content of the wood. So the measurements would be of dimensions of the beam under test, loads applied, deformation of the wood, and temperature and moisture content.

From all this, knowing something of how you might expect the wood to behave, you would use mathematical, particularly statistical, methods to find the interrelation between the measurements and other phenomena such as crushing loads, bending and shear properties.

> **The subject of statistics is important because the measurements you make are imperfect.**

All measurements are imperfect; it is no reflection on you. Consider measuring the length of a room with a tape measure that is 30 metres long. You can never measure it exactly right for a number of reasons: your inability to hold both ends of the tape in exactly the right place, your inability to read the tape exactly when interpolating between the marks on the tape, using an incorrectly calibrated tape, incorrectly measuring the temperature to take account of the thermal expansion of the tape, holding the tape at an incorrect tension, etc.

Now, if you and some friends measured the length of a room with different tapes on different days under different conditions and came up with these measurements: 23.456 m, 23.482 m, 23.471 m, 12.135 m and 23.463 m, what would be the true length of the room? Discounting the obvious blunder of 12.135 m, there are still four measurements that are equally valid but all different.

	23.456 m
	23.482 m
	23.471 m
	23.463 m
mean	23.468 m

As good an estimate of the true value of the length of the room as any would be to take the mean, 23.468 m. How close this is to the truth is impossible to say, but statistics will allow you to calculate a measure of the uncertainty of the mean of your four good measurements.

The point is that if your measurements are all wrong, how can you draw any firm conclusions? OK, that's a bit harsh, but let's just admit that your measurements have uncertain errors. The answer is that you cannot draw absolute conclusions. But since you can calculate the uncertainty of your measurements you can use that information to calculate the uncertainty of your conclusions. So you *can* draw imperfect conclusions from imperfect measurements. More importantly, you can estimate uncertainty, and hence the significance of your conclusions.

You can recognise quantitative methods as those which involve some or all of the following:

■ creating mathematical models to investigate theories and hypotheses;

■ designing instruments;

■ developing methods of measurement;

■ collecting numerical data;

■ experiments with controls;

■ changing variables and appraising the results.

Quantitative research can be a cyclical process. You start with an idea, a working hypothesis, and conduct an experiment by making measurements and drawing conclusions. The conclusions lead you to reconsider and alter your hypothesis and so you conduct another experiment etc., as in Figure 3.2.

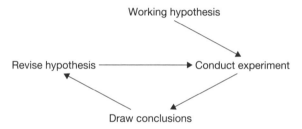

Figure 3.2 Research as a cyclical process

3.7.2 Qualitative methods

Qualitative research is rather different from quantitative research in that it is concerned with ideas, opinions, meanings and perceptions. This is rather more difficult for scientists and engineers whose understanding of the world is often reflected in numbers and formulae. For us, qualitative research is most useful as a means of creating hypotheses, rather than finding the values of parameters by statistical means.

This can be particularly useful if we do not understand or cannot identify the question we are seeking to answer. For example, if some buildings in a town have collapsed there could be a number of possible root causes. Possibly there are geological or geotechnical problems associated with the ground conditions. It may be that there are defects in the design of the buildings. Alternatively, perhaps faulty materials have been used during construction. So before undertaking any technical research into the problem it would be necessary to identify which of these, if any, may be the cause.

Qualitative research might help to identify the problem. The methods of qualitative research are typically those of direct observation by the researcher, questionnaire or interview, and document review.

- By direct observation the researcher may see if there have been landslips or subsidence in the area.

- If the researcher interviews the construction workers and the engineers involved it may be possible to identify whether faulty materials had a part to play.

- On looking at geological maps it may become apparent that the collapse of underground mine workings could have caused subsidence.

- A study of construction plans and calculations may raise concern about any inadequacy of the design.

A 'case study' is the most likely place that you might use qualitative research. Often a question is posed and, following research, quantitative or qualitative, results are obtained and some tentative conclusions drawn. Those conclusions may then be illustrated or otherwise by undertaking a case study.

> **Be very careful about drawing firm conclusions from case studies as those conclusions are only valid for the case being studied.**

Case studies may give deep insight, but only within the limited scope of the case concerned.

The way to broaden your conclusions is to study a number of partially related cases to see if there are more general conclusions to be drawn. So, if in biology you are investigating some aspect of a particular grass in a meadow in Cornwall, see if you can also study the same grass on a hillside in Worcestershire and a dale in Yorkshire. If the same phenomena appear in all three cases, under different conditions of climate, topography and altitude, you will come to a more general and therefore a more useful conclusion.

Remember that a case study is only valid as contributing to your research if you have carried out the case study yourself. If you intend merely to report on a case study carried out by others, for example on something you have found on the internet, then it would probably be more appropriate to include that in the literature review.

● 3.8 Getting the data

Whether you are going to use qualitative or quantitative methods you will need some data to work with. You will have to identify the data you need to be able to achieve your objectives, and hence your aim, and you will also need to identify how you are going to get those data and subsequently how you are going to analyse them.

Data are often thought of as being either primary or secondary.

> **In essence, primary data are data you collect yourself and secondary data are those which have been collected by others.**

If you set up an experiment to investigate how variations in the quantity of an additive affect the crushing strength of concrete then the experiment is yours, the observations are yours and so the data are yours. If in astronomy you have made observations to a quasar (quasi-stellar object) and recorded the radio signals from it then those are your own observations. In both cases you have primary data.

The advantages of primary data are that you know exactly what you have and the data contain only what you need. The disadvantage is that the data are often hard to win and because you have to set up experiments or do fieldwork this may take time, money and possibly risk. See Table 3.1.

Table 3.1 Primary and secondary data

Data	For	Against
Primary	You know the data well The data contains only what you need	Data are hard to win Collection may take time Cost Risk of failure
Secondary	Usually quicker and easier to get	Uncertain accuracy May not be complete May not be systematic Need to determine reliability

Another source of primary data is data from questionnaires and interviews, as long as you send out the questionnaires or conduct the interviews. There is more about questionnaires and interviews in the following sections.

If you seek to investigate some aspect of zoology, geology or railway engineering in Kenya then an extensive, expensive and possibly uncertain field trip will be required. If you do have such an enterprise in mind then discuss your ideas with your tutor first before getting carried away with planning or parting with money. It is unlikely that you will get any financial support from your institution but your tutors might know of a source of support.

On the other hand, if you are an overseas student or live on an interesting but remote island and get the opportunity to collect data on a trip back home, you could end up with a project that is distinctly different from those of your peers. Alternatively, you might combine an overseas holiday with the data-gathering exercise. Make sure you get your priorities right if you do so. Data collection will almost certainly take more time than you anticipated and there is always the danger of coming back with insufficient or incomplete data to do a meaningful project.

Do not confuse work with pleasure.

However, if this is what you want to do then discuss it with your tutor first and plan to collect the data on a holiday before the project formally starts. If it all goes wrong then you will have time to think of an alternative project.

Secondary data are those that were previously collected by others and therefore are generally quicker and possibly easier to get. You may be able to identify sources from professional or trade associations, published government statistics or even data collected by previous students or researchers working in the same area.

Beware! Before even thinking of using secondary data, first ask why those data were collected and by whom.

What you are really trying to establish is whether the data are suitable for your investigation. You need to assess how accurate, how complete, how systematic and how reliable the data are and so decide if they really are going to be useful in helping you answer your question. Think carefully about any secondary data that you propose to use; there are a lot of questions in that last sentence.

If you are collecting only quantitative data by experiment or fieldwork and definitely do not intend to consider questionnaires or interviews, omit the rest of this chapter and go to Chapter 4 now.

3.9 Questionnaires

Using questionnaires or interviews is an excellent way of getting primary qualitative data. However, to get good quality and a good quantity of data you will need to do some careful planning. This section will help you to manage your use of questionnaires and the next section, your interviews. The two methods are not mutually exclusive and it may be appropriate to use both questionnaires and interviews.

Writing a good questionnaire is more art than science.

You need to consider what information you want to get and how you are going to analyse it. You need to identify your target audience and the means of delivery to that audience. But above all you will have to compose your questionnaire so that each potential respondent will be persuaded to reply fully and honestly, rather than just throw it in the wastepaper bin or delete it from the email inbox.

You will need to select the right people to send your questionnaire to and write it in such a way that they will respond. If you get a 30% return you are doing very well indeed! A poorly constructed questionnaire may get only a few returns. People are more likely to reply if they think the investigation is worthy of support and they are knowledgeable and interested in the subject.

A short questionnaire is more likely to be returned.

You can increase the likelihood of a return by keeping the questionnaire short enough that it takes no more than 30 minutes to complete. The instructions and questions should be clear and unambiguous. The questionnaire should have a professional look to give it the appearance of integrity. Use plenty of white space and no more than two fonts. Try to keep each question to 20 words or fewer. Long questions can be confusing. Check boxes should be lined up to the right of the page for consistency and ease of use by respondents, who will be mostly right-handed.

Briefly explain the purpose of the questionnaire in a covering letter and say what you intend to do with the results. If you are going to ask personal or sensitive questions, make sure there is no way that the reply can be traced back to the respondent and state in your letter that all replies will be anonymous and individual replies will be treated with confidence. That of course means that you must not include such replies in an appendix to your dissertation.

If you can also include a reply-paid envelope it will indicate that you are committed to the research and it also invites the respondent to be committed as well.

If you are permitted to include your tutor's phone or email contact details (ask first or this could backfire on you) then that will also add to the appearance of integrity of your questionnaire.

If the rate of return is poor you might send out a reminder, after a month, say, enclosing another copy of the questionnaire in case the original has been lost. A second reminder is unlikely to bring in many more returns. If you have promised anonymity and not included contact details then you will have to send the reminder to all those on the original list with a note of apology in case they have already responded.

Another way of encouraging a greater rate of return, especially if there is only a limited number of people to whom it would be appropriate to send your questionnaire in the first place, is to make contact by phone or email first. Explain your purpose and ask if they would be prepared to take part in your survey. If you get a positive response you could email the questionnaire immediately and, with a bit of luck, may get the reply within a few hours.

If your respondent does not return the completed questionnaire as expected, you then have the opportunity to send a gentle reminder.

> **Always remember that your respondents are doing you a favour. Politeness, consideration, patience, understanding and, above all, gratitude are of the essence.**

'Brevity is the soul of wit' wrote Shakespeare, but it is doubtful if he sent out many questionnaires. If he did, they would have been short, to the point and well phrased. It is not difficult to write a good questionnaire provided you follow the following guidelines.

There are different types of questions you can ask. An open question lets the respondents reply as they wish, in a few words or as a long narrative. A closed question is one where the choice of answers is limited. For example:

> Open question – How well is safety managed in your laboratory?
>
> Closed question – Which do you think best describes how safety is managed in your laboratory?
>
> a) Well, b) Adequately, c) Poorly, d) Don't know

With an open question it is up to you to interpret the answer and draw meaning from the disparate answers. With a closed question the respondent makes the assessment and so you may group replies more easily. Open questions require more work by the respondent but the answers may offer up more insight. Closed questions are easier and quicker to answer.

In asking a closed question you might want to offer your respondent a scale of replies to select from. One way is invite the respondent to select an appropriate strength of agreement to a proposition.

> Career opportunities for chemists working in the petrochemical industry have increased in the last 10 years.
>
> Strongly agree, Agree, No change, Disagree, Strongly disagree

The five-point scale is commonly used. Any more points and the choice may become ambiguous; fewer points leave little room for expressing a strength or weakness of opinion. Whether there should be a neutral option, i.e. the 'no change' above, is questionable. To have a neutral option allows those with no opinion to express their absence of opinion. On the other hand, leaving out the neutral or 'no opinion' option forces respondents to make choices by not letting them sit on the fence. You will need to consider your target audience; are they likely to be strong minded, or do they need help forming an opinion?

An alternative is to put the neutral or 'no opinion' option at the end of the list of options rather than in the middle. Such a placing makes the neutral option appear as a secondary alternative and may persuade some respondents to opt for one of the more constructive choices.

A scale of opinion like that above lends itself to scoring the responses, e.g. strongly agree = 1 to strongly disagree = 5. Such a simple numerical conversion from a qualitative

Table 3.2 Questions in matrix form

Tick the appropriate boxes	Strongly agree	Agree	Not sure	Disagree	Strongly disagree
Solar heating is effective in colder climates					
Solar heating installation is economical					
Solar panels on domestic roofs are unsightly					

to a quantitative response will make the data more amenable to statistical analysis, providing that the numerical scale values are valid.

If a series of questions follows the same format, with the same range of responses, then it may be easier for the respondent to reply if the questions are in a matrix form. See Table 3.2. It will also be easier for you to collate and analyse the results.

Anything you can do to make the questionnaire easy to answer will increase your chances of success. Avoid making your respondents having to think where you can do it for them.

Likewise, avoid specific personal questions. If you need to ask about salaries, for example, rather than ask 'What is your current salary?' give a range of options to choose from, e.g. in units of £, $ or €, and invite the respondent to select the appropriate range from: less than 10K, 10K–20K, 20K–40K, 40K–80K, greater than 80K. After all, it is likely that you will have little interest in anyone's exact reply and you will later have to put the replies into groups, so this type of question will do that part of the work for you as well.

Avoid irrelevant questions. A 'contingency question' is a two-part question where the answer to the first part directs the respondent to the next relevant question. Respondents may be frustrated and alienated by questions that clearly do not apply to them. There is an example in Figure 3.3, again in the context of laboratory health and safety.

How would you feel about being asked the wrong question from 2 and 3 in Figure 3.3?

In your questions you may be looking for facts, beliefs and opinions, attitudes or behaviour. Facts are statements of truth. To each question there is only one true

---

1. Are you male or female? Circle one.　　　　Male　　　　Female

　　If female, go to question 2. If male, go to question 3.

2. Are there appropriate facilities for the disposal of sanitary towels in your toilets?

　　Yes / No.................... Now go to question 4

3. Are there sufficient urinals in your toilets?

　　Yes / No.................... Now go to question 4

4. What do you think of ...

Figure 3.3 Contingency question

answer. A belief is something held to be true even if it is not so. The question asks about your perception of, not the truth of, the situation. An attitude is a state of mind influenced by feelings and values. Behavioural questions seek to find out what the respondent would do, or does, or did do in a given situation. You need to be clear in your mind what kind of question it is that you are asking because it will affect the kind of answer you get.

Factual question
How old are you?

Belief/opinion question
Do you think that the cleaners are sufficiently aware of the potential hazards in the laboratory?

Attitude question
How do you feel about the quality of medical cover in case of emergency in the laboratory? A) Confident B) Unsure

Behavioural question
What would you do if a fire broke out in the laboratory?

Each question should be directly relevant to the research you are carrying out. You should not pad out the questionnaire with superfluous questions. Asking about the colour of a piece of equipment has little relevance if it is the performance characteristics you need to know about.

Avoid asking questions that the respondent is unlikely to be able to answer. A physics researcher may know nothing of a software package used in biological research. Likewise, what might a chemist know of civil engineering contract procedures?

Do not ask unnecessary questions.

Also avoid asking personal or emotive questions. If you do not need to know the respondent's salary, age, marital status, political opinions or religion, for example, don't ask.

Keep the questions simple to avoid ambiguity or accidentally asking double questions. What kind of response would you expect to 'Should trams, buses and taxis in the city centre be free for students and the elderly?' This is actually six questions in one and will be thoroughly confusing for the respondent and so the replies will be full of ambiguity. It would be better to ask:

Should trams in the city centre be free for students?	Yes /No
Should buses in the city centre be free for students?	Yes /No
Should taxis in the city centre be free for students?	Yes /No
Should trams in the city centre be free for the elderly?	Yes /No
Should buses in the city centre be free for the elderly?	Yes /No
Should taxis in the city centre be free for the elderly?	Yes /No

---

Leading questions elicit biased answers. For example, the question 'Don't you think that it is true that nuclear physicists are overpaid?' invites you to side with the argument that nuclear physicists *are* overpaid and so only the nuclear physicists are likely to disagree.

The order of the questions needs some consideration. There is no absolutely right way to do this. It is probably best to start with the simple, factual, non-threatening questions. Scale questions are easy to answer and make respondents feel they are making good progress in getting through the paperwork. It is probably better not to have all the open-ended questions together as they can be tiring because they may require deep or emotive thought and there is then a danger that the questionnaire will be abandoned.

As much as possible, your questions should flow naturally. The answer to one question should not be swayed by the answer to any earlier question. It is better to have the more general questions at the beginning and then lead on to more specific ones. Have any sensitive questions towards the end. Overall, start with the factual questions then lead to questions about behaviour and finally to questions requiring attitude or opinion.

> **Sensitive questions should be left until last.**

Before including a sensitive question, ask yourself if it is really necessary to ask it. If there are to be sensitive questions, make it clear in the instructions that all questions do not have to be answered. It is better to have a partly completed questionnaire returned than not at all.

On the other hand, if it is essential for your survey to ask a sensitive question to which you almost certainly get no reply or a potentially untrue one, such as 'Has your boss ever asked you to dump toxic substances from the laboratory down the sink?', then you could reduce your respondent's potential difficulty by including a random response.

For example, ask the respondent to toss a coin before answering. If it comes down heads, unknown to you of course, then the reply is to be 'yes', whether it is true or not. If the coin comes down tails answer truthfully. This way it is not possible to tell if the sensitive 'yes' answer is true or a result of the randomising process. What can be deduced from the overall set of replies is that if there are 70% 'yes' replies then 50% are as a result of the randomising process and 20% are true. Therefore the real number of true 'yes' answers is twice the apparent 20%, i.e. 40%.

Finally, at the bottom of the questionnaire, say 'thank you'.

So now you have written your questionnaire, identified the intended recipients, and are ready to send it out. How can you be sure of a good number of returns? The first step is to ask two or three friends who also know something about writing questionnaires and whom you can trust to be critically constructive to review it.

> **Next, conduct a pilot study by sending out the questionnaire to about 10–20% of your target audience.**

You will then get some idea of the percentage return you can expect and so may identify the need to expand your mailing list if the return is poor. By studying the returns you will see which questions are not well answered and you may be able to work out why. For example, the questions may be intrusive, vague or ambiguous, or may require a full open answer when you have just given a yes/no option. If that occurs you will have the opportunity to revise those questions or even delete them if they are not essential.

Your institution or your tutor may require that you get approval before sending out questionnaires.

If you and a number of your friends intend sending questionnaires to the same people you are not likely to get many replies. Most professional people are very busy and although many, but not most, will be prepared to take the time to complete one questionnaire the majority will feel used, if not abused, to be asked to complete several from the same institution, especially if the questionnaires are asking similar questions.

As part of your analysis of the replies try to identify any groups of your target recipients where there were particularly poor or non-existent returns and see if you can work out why that was so. You should comment on this in your analysis of results.

3.10 Interviews

Interviews are an alternative way of getting similar data to that achieved by question-naires. The big advantage of the interview is that of near certainty of response, once you have got the interview that is, and the ability to develop any unexpected themes that crop up in discussion. Of course, one cost is that of getting yourself to the interview, a cost in both money and time. You will also need time to identify potential interviewees and arrange the interviews.

Alternatively, the interview may be conducted by telephone, but although a face-to-face interview may last from 30 minutes to one hour, a telephone interview is likely to be much shorter. Since you and the interviewee do not have to meet, your respondents can be drawn from across the country, if not the world.

Telephone interviews are probably the fastest way of capturing data. However, it is much more difficult to establish trust or rapport in a short telephone conversation, especially if the interviewee does not know you, so be patient when explaining the purpose and importance of your research. It is very unlikely that you can ask sensitive questions over the telephone.

The preparation for the interview is similar to that of the questionnaire in terms of planning what data you need to collect and how you are going to get them. Interviews should be structured and focused. If the interviewee feels that time is being wasted then the interview may be cut short.

One reason for having a fixed structure for your interview is to ensure that you ask the same questions, in the same order and in the same way, to all your interviewees.

A problem that could occur with an interview may be that of clash of personality between you and your interviewee. You will need to ensure that your interviewee is at ease with you. This may be difficult if you, a student, are interviewing a senior person in your industry.

If your interview contains a lot of open-ended questions and none are sensitive or personal you might ask the interviewee for permission to record the interview.

No hidden microphones, remember the ethics!

If the interview is recorded then you can transcribe the relevant parts later and you will not make mistakes or miss important parts while note taking. On the other hand, if your recording device fails during the interview you will have nothing but your memory to fall back on. Be aware that some interviewees may feel obliged to agree to the recording but do so reluctantly and therefore give limited responses to your questions. There is a delicate balance of judgement required here which you will need to make on the day.

A focus group is a form of semi-unstructured collective interview. In this the interviewer takes the role of a moderator and explores issues with a group taken from the target population. Just as with interviews, it is essential to prepare a list of questions to be answered. The difficulty with a focus group is in keeping the group focused on the questions that you, the researcher/moderator, want answered. It is also difficult to equate the outcome of one focus group with that of another even though it is drawn from the same target population and addressing the same question.

In conclusion to this section, a face-to-face interview lets you have a rapport with your interviewee and allows you to observe as well as listen. A telephone interview costs less to conduct in time and money and so is appropriate when there are relatively few questions and they are simple. Data gathering by questionnaire is slow but cheap and can be used to get data from larger groups who could not all be interviewed in the same period of time.

● 3.11 Summary

- Health and safety are paramount. You should follow your institution's guidance and procedures.

- Ensure that your project meets ethical standards.

- Your imperfect measurements lead to imperfect conclusions. Few measurements are perfect; there is little you can do about that.

- Research methods are generally quantitative or qualitative.

- Quantitative research is concerned with investigating problems that can be represented by numbers.

- Quantitative methods involve mathematical modelling, designing instruments, developing methods of measurement, collecting numerical data and experiments with controls.

- Qualitative research is concerned with ideas, opinions, meanings and perceptions and is useful for understanding or identifying problems.

- Qualitative research tools are direct observation, questionnaire, interview and document review.

- Case studies may give deep insight, but only of the case concerned.

- Primary data are what you collect, but they may be expensive to get.

- Secondary data are collected by others but they may not be accurate, complete, systematic or reliable.

- Questionnaires and interviews are excellent ways of getting primary qualitative data.

- Writing a good questionnaire will take time and thought.
- Explain the purpose of your questionnaire; keep it brief and well structured.
- Think of the best way of asking each question: open or closed, whether to use a scale and how to present it, matrix questions, contingency questions, factual, belief/opinion, attitude or behavioural questions.
- Keep questions directly relevant, impersonal, non-sensitive and simple.
- The order of the questions is important.
- Conduct a pilot study.
- Thoroughly plan your interviews and have a fixed structure.

What next?

Check your institution's health and safety requirements.

Complete a risk assessment for your project according to your institution's requirements.

Check your institution's guidelines for ethical research. Make sure you conform.

You will have to decide whether your data are to be qualitative or quantitative. If they are only quantitative, go to the next chapter.

Decide what qualitative data you need to capture.

Decide whether you are going to use primary or secondary data.

If they are to be primary qualitative data, decide whether they are best collected by face-to-face interview, telephone interview, questionnaire or document examination.

If you use questionnaires or interviews, write out all your questions and select the order.

Consider using case studies.

Conduct a pilot study and modify your questionnaire or interview accordingly.

Conduct your survey.

CHAPTER
4

Meaning from numbers

You may collect data or undertake an experiment.

Either way your results will appear as a set of numbers. How do you make sense of it all? It is most unlikely that the analysis will be simple and clear cut and yet you will have to come to some meaningful and justifiable conclusions. If you can easily arrive at unambiguous conclusions it is likely that either your investigation was superficial or you have not extracted all the meaning that is hidden within the numbers.

The aim of this chapter is to aid you in extracting logical meaning from the data that you collect while undertaking your project. By the end of this chapter you should be able to:

- **Appreciate the nature of uncertainty and the different types of data you might be using.**

- **Understand the importance of taking a common-sense view of your data before applying statistical processes to it.**

- **Recognise where to apply the different statistical processes involved with parametric and non-parametric methods.**

This is not a statistics textbook; there is simply not enough space here to cover everything there is to know about the design and analysis of experiments.

This chapter will bring to your attention some of the issues you should consider when planning your data capture, analysing the results and drawing meaning from the analysis. There are many good statistics textbooks and you should use these to look up specific methods and formulae.

For a fuller description of this subject see:

Barnard, C., Gilbert, F. and McGregor, P. (2007) *Asking question in biology: A guide to hypothesis testing, experimental design and presentation in practical work and research projects* (3rd edition), Benjamin Cummings, Harlow.

Montgomery, D. (2008) *Design and analysis of experiments* (7th edition), John Wiley & Sons, Hoboken, NJ, USA.

Weiss, N. (2007) *Elementary statistics* (7th edition), Addison Wesley, Harlow.

4.1 The nature of uncertainty

Uncertainty may look like your enemy, but valid conclusions can be drawn from the most unpromising of data. To do this you will use statistical methods. Discrete measurements may be exact; there are three people in the room, say, never 3.1 or 2.9. One discrete measurement alone will be coarse and lacking in information about the quality of that measurement.

On the other hand, no single continuous measurement is ever correct. Even over a very small range there will be an infinite number of possibilities. If you are measuring the length of a field then someone else may also measure the same distance under the same conditions just as accurately as you, but come up with a slightly different value. The same applies whether the measurement is of a lunar distance with an earth-based laser-ranger to targets on the moon or the measurement of the size of a cell under a microscope.

If it were possible to make a single measurement that answered the research question of your project then there would be no need for this chapter. However, you would probably have a project that was so trivial that it would not even be worth thinking about, let alone doing.

In your project you will have accumulated data. Some of the data may be in the form of measurements and so will be highly numerical and some of it may be in the form of surveys and interviews and may not be so numerical.

> **Your task now is to extract meaning from the data in the form of results, which lead to conclusions.**

Most of your final results will be in terms of representative values with assessments of their spread, uncertainty, quality and correlations. Statistics, which as a subject is the mathematics of uncertainty, is the route to achieving your goals. A statistic, in the singular, is just a number with meaning.

'There are lies, damned lies and statistics' is a quotation that has been attributed to Mark Twain and to Benjamin Disraeli. It is not known who said it first, if either, so before we even start, there is an example of uncertainty. Since statistics is about uncertainty it is quite possible for two people to draw different meanings from the same data depending upon how they treat it. Whatever you do, it must be rigorously justifiable if your tutor is not going to find fault with your method.

● 4.2 Data types

Data may be nominal, ordinal, interval or ratio. Data are nominal when there is no obvious order to the categories, for example in a questionnaire you are asked to tick from a list the factors that made you choose your course or your job.

With ordinal data the categories are in a meaningful sequence and are related to each other. If you were asked to select from a list which height range you are in, 1.6–1.7 m, 1.7–1.8 m, 1.8–1.9 m etc., the data would be ordinal.

Interval data may have numerical values but have no obvious zero point or consistent scale. If you were asked to put a numerical value to your satisfaction with your job/course on a range of 1 for very satisfied to 5 for very dissatisfied then a score of zero would not be meaningful. Also, the difference between 2 and 3 might not be the same as the difference between 4 and 5.

Variables are ratio when an obvious zero point exists and the intervals between the categories are the same. Most numerical experimental data in science and engineering are of this form. Discrete ratio variables can only take specific values such as the number of eggs in a bird's nest; there can only be 0 or 1 or 2 or 3 etc., never 1.6 or 2.34. Continuous ratio variables can take any values within the applicable range and there are, theoretically, an infinite number of possibilities; a piece of metal may weigh 1.2 kg or 1.237 kg or 1.23725 kg, provided you have the instrumentation to measure to that level of accuracy. Practically every experimental measurement you make involving time, length, mass, temperature, electric current, angle or any quantity that combines any of these, e.g. force, will be a continuous ratio variable.

● 4.3 Previewing your data

There are many statistical tests that you can perform on your data but the best first test is just to take a look at the data to see if there are any obvious anomalies or interesting but unexpected features that should be investigated. By way of example, here is a set of marks, maximum 100, for a first year science or engineering mathematics examination, a data set that is likely to have meaning to all readers of this book. These marks are the raw data:

68, 45, 94, 68, 44, 7, 62, 45, 73, 77, 45, 17, 70, 42, 77, 64, 47, 37, 84, 48, 80, 72, 46, 7, 76, 48, 68, 86, 52, 7, 46, 44, 55, 72, 43, 1, 87, 49, 61, 92, 39, 7, 71, 38, 76, 55, 42, 0, 67, 45, 49, 71, 49, 19, 72, 48, 81, 66, 45, 1, 94, 49, 64, 76, 43, 10, 65, 45, 65, 75, 45, 11, 72, 35, 67, 70, 43, 1, 85, 38, 62, 60, 54, 5, 66, 47, 70, 68, 49, 22, 53, 45, 6, 75, 44, 1, 64, 54, 1, 79

Of itself this presents little obvious information. A quick scan across the numbers reveals some good marks and some that are not so good. A simple calculation of mean and standard deviation reveals values of 51 and 25 respectively. The low mean would be disappointing, given that the pass mark is 40%, and the large standard deviation might suggest a wide range of abilities in the group. If the marks are now grouped into classes of 0, 1–5, 6–10, 11–15, . . . 91–95 and 96–100 and the frequency in each class plotted at the class mid-points of 0, 3, 8, 13 etc. then the data, when plotted as in Figure 4.1, reveal a rather different story.

Just a glance at the graph indicates that the distribution is far from a normal distribution. Indeed there appear to be three rather separate groups, each of which might, but not necessarily, be normally distributed. The group with scores over 58 have little to worry about, but the middle group, with a mode at 43, are doing little more than

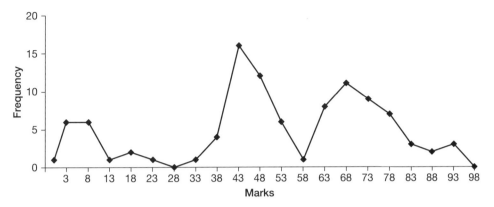

Figure 4.1 Mathematics marks grouped as data

straddle the pass/fail border line. There is a third but smaller group at the lower end of the graph.

The fact that the data show such an interesting distribution leads to many questions. Why do sub-groups appear in this population? Are there correlations between marks and other factors such as age, gender, part- or full-time study or previous mathematical qualifications? Investigations might lead the course tutors to draw conclusions on how to further the education of the three groups and possibly lead to decisions relating to revising the admissions criteria for future students.

> **Notice how this review of the data, through a graphical representation, has drawn out substantial meaning but without any formal statistical analysis.**

Previewing the data may help to resolve issues associated with 'outliers'. Outliers are measurements that do not fit with the rest of the set for some as yet unexplained reason. They may exist because the distribution is not normal and there are factors which have yet to be accounted for, as in the last example, or there are mistakes in the data. Mistakes can occur for a variety of reasons such as:

> Misreading instruments – e.g. parallax error when reading an analogue thermometer at an oblique angle.
>
> Procedural errors – e.g. recording air temperature with the thermometer in direct sunlight.
>
> Incorrectly recording observations – e.g. writing down a temperature of 37.4 °C when the reading was 27.4 °C.
>
> Data transcription errors – e.g. entering 12.3 into a spreadsheet for a temperature in degrees Celsius when it should have been 13.2.

Often a simple graphical plot will indicate the presence of significant outliers. You will then have to decide what you should do with them; for example, should you remove them from your data set? If they are there because of straightforward blunders in measurement or data transcription, then the erroneous observations must be removed. Failure to do so will lead to erroneous results and hence erroneous conclusions.

If the measurements can be trusted, then the outliers indicate un-modelled phenomena that require further investigation. There are different ways of examining a data set for outliers. If it can be confirmed that there are no un-modelled phenomena, and therefore all outliers are blunders, then those outliers that are a significant number of standard deviations from the mean may be rejected. Deciding how many standard deviations are significant will probably depend upon experience in the context of your experiment or field data.

For example, if as a moderately experienced experimenter you know that you make mistakes in about 1 in 20 of your observations then it is reasonable to exclude the least well fitting 5% of your observations on the basis that they are probably blunders. In the normal distribution 95% of observations will fit within approximately ± 2 standard deviations of the mean. However, beware of blindly following the statistics; the following example illustrates why.

Here is a set of measurements of the weight of a single sample taken under the same conditions by the same person. There is every reason to suppose that only random variations should apply.

9.573, 9.595, 9.575, 9.634, 9.576, 9.537, 9.574, 9.572 kg

Ranked in order these become:

9.537, 9.572, 9.573, 9.574, 9.575, 9.576, 9.595, 9.634 kg

The data are plotted as a dot plot (Figure 4.2), with markers at the mean and ± 2 standard deviations (σ) shown.

One of the observations is just outside the ± 2 standard deviations limits and so is rejected as a blunder. A new mean and standard deviation are calculated with the reduced data set and the results similarly plotted (Figure 4.3).

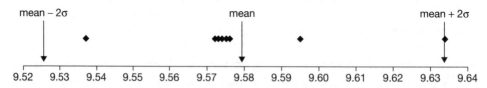

Figure 4.2 Dot plot of all weight measurements

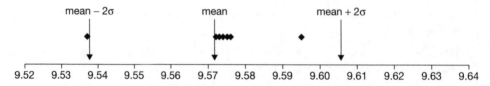

Figure 4.3 Dot plot of seven weight measurements

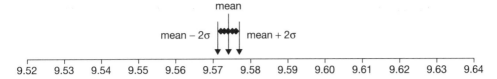

Figure 4.4 Dot plot of remaining five weight measurements

Again, one of the observations is just outside the ± 2 standard deviations range and so is rejected as a blunder. A new mean and standard deviation are calculated with the reduced data set and the results similarly plotted. Yet again one of the observations is just outside the new ± 2 standard deviations range and so the exercise is repeated. Now there are just 5 observations left and since all are within ± 2 standard deviations of the mean they are accepted. See Figure 4.4.

By following the statistics, you have now removed almost 40% of your observations. From the data above, the standard deviations for the first and last tests were 0.027 and 0.002 kg respectively; a vast difference. It might have been better to estimate the standard deviations of your observations from experience before conducting the experiment and use that value to determine your rejection criteria.

Beware of pruning your data excessively by removing too many outliers. Each time you reject another outlier the standard deviation of the remaining data set gets smaller and so the data set appears to get better. This is only the case if the rejected data really are blunders and not just large random errors. This can be a difficult judgement to make.

Here is another example where you could be misled by statistics. Let's say you conduct an experiment to investigate the effect of temperature upon yield in a chemical or biological process. A raw plot of the data is in Figure 4.5.

The correlation coefficient of this data is 0.44, which suggests a strong, although far from absolute correlation between yield and temperature. Any coefficient of correlation

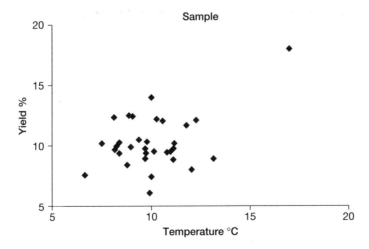

Figure 4.5 Yield against temperature

always lies between +1 and −1. A coefficient of +1 indicates that there is a fixed and positive relationship between yield and temperature. If that were the case then all the points would lie on a straight line that had a positive gradient. A coefficient of −1 indicates a fixed and negative relationship and so all the points would lie on a straight line with a negative gradient.

Figure 4.5 shows that there is one potential outlier at the top right of the graph. If this suspect observation is removed from the data set then the coefficient of correlation is reduced to 0.03. A coefficient of correlation of zero indicates that there is no relationship between yield and temperature. The removal of one suspect observation has changed the conclusion that would be derived from this experiment from strong correlation to almost no correlation at all.

So, data must be viewed and investigated before statistical processes are applied to them. A good look, preferably in graphical form, may help to prevent you from applying statistical processes to inappropriate data and so drawing false conclusions.

● 4.4 Statistical methods

The nature of your data will dictate how you can analyse them. Statistical methods are said to be parametric or non-parametric. The term 'parametric' refers to measures of the central tendency and to measures of the dispersion or spread of the data, for example the mean and standard deviation of the set respectively. Parametric statistics are most usefully applied to continuous ratio variables but less easily applied to the analysis of other forms of data. For example, you could not find the mean of a set of reasons for liking your job/course, let alone find a standard deviation of those reasons; it just does not make sense. Non-parametric methods are usually more applicable for variables that are not of the continuous ratio type.

Any experiment or field data collection will be in three stages: the design, the data collection and the analysis. The analysis should lead to meaningful conclusions and so the design must ensure that this is possible.

Your statistical method may be in the form of hypothesis testing leading to the determination of significance in your results or may just be in the determination of measures of uncertainty in your results; either way, the simpler you can keep the statistical process the easier it will be to perform.

● 4.5 Parametric methods

Most experimentation and fieldwork will use parametric methods.

Let's say you wished to investigate the effect of two possible additives on the curing time for concrete. Your experiment might therefore involve making a series of cubes of concrete, with and without the additives, at different temperatures and measuring their crushing strengths after different periods of time.

You now have a series of decisions to make. What differences in curing times would be of consequence? What level of result would be statistically significant? How precisely can you make your measurements of crushing strength? How consistently can you replicate the concrete mix, the proportion of additive and the curing conditions, especially temperature? These decisions will lead you to selecting the number of replications of each combination of proportion of additive and time of curing.

It may be tempting to try to investigate a larger number of factors rather than just the two, additive and curing time, described above. Each new factor adds another layer of complexity to the experimental design and it is easy to propose something that becomes so large and complex that it is impossible to complete in the time you have available. You will need to hold some factors as fixed and accept that your work is limited to the conditions specified by those factors. At the very least this will lead to some recommendations for further work where those factors can be varied.

You will need to ensure that the order in which you conduct your trials is random so that you guard against any unintended time-related bias coming into the process. Replications should be blocked to ensure that un-modelled factors, such as variability in the consistency of the concrete mix from different suppliers, are averaged out.

Each of the variables in this experiment may be characterised by a statistical distribution. If the distribution is 'normal' then the distribution is fully described by the parameters of its mean (μ) and standard deviation (σ). By knowing how the normal distribution behaves and knowing the parameters of a particular variable we can predict how the variable will behave.

4.6 Non-parametric methods

Non-parametric methods will need to be used where assumptions about distributions are incorrect or inappropriate. Whereas parametric methods will most often be used where there is numerical measurement such as in experiments, non-parametric methods will find most favour in the analysis of questionnaires and interviews.

For example, if the options for the reply to a question are: Strongly agree; Agree; No/neutral opinion; Disagree; Strongly disagree, how will you analyse the data? If you convert these responses into numerical equivalents of 5, 4, 3, 2 and 1, respectively, you have made the assumption that the difference between Strongly agree and No/neutral opinion is the same as the difference between No/neutral opinion and Strongly disagree. Likewise, does Agree have twice the value of Disagree? It is unlikely that such assumptions are valid; that is, you do not have interval-type data.

To analyse such data requires non-parametric methods. There is often more than one non-parametric method equivalent to each parametric method. For example, the 'Student's *t*-test' for differences between groups has the corresponding Kolmogorov–Smirnov test, the Mann–Whitney U or Wilcoxon rank sum test, and the Wald–Wolfowitz runs test; depending upon which is more appropriate for the data.

First, examine the nature of your data. Consult a textbook on, or containing material about, non-parametric statistics and then select the appropriate tests to use. Alternatively, links to non-parametric tests may be found under 'Non-parametric statistics' in the Wikipedia encyclopaedia at http://en.wikipedia.org/wiki/Non-parametric_statistics. Care should be taken when using this site as the content is not subject to rigorous review and technical content should be confirmed in textbooks or on other sites.

4.7 Summary

- Experimental data are mostly continuous.
- Measurements always contain error. With careful design and conduct of the experiment or fieldwork those errors should only be random.
- Statistical methods allow you to draw meaningful conclusions at appropriate levels of significance.
- Although data may be nominal, ordinal, interval or ratio, most experimental data are ratio but some qualitative data may be nominal or ordinal.
- Always preview your data before applying statistical techniques. Preview in a visual way where possible, perhaps by using graphs.
- Be wary of blindly following statistical procedures when rejecting doubtful data.
- It is worth spending time carefully designing your experiment or fieldwork collection. If the data are inadequate, no amount of sophisticated statistics will compensate for it.

What next?

Make sure your experiment, fieldwork or survey is well designed to ensure that meaningful results can be obtained.

Ensure you are conversant with the statistical methods you will need to employ. If you are not, now is the time to read up about statistical methods.

Collect your data, extract the results and perform the analysis.

Paperwork, paperwork

Hopefully you have decided to write up your dissertation as you go along.

It is so much easier to create your text as you work through each stage than to make notes and then hope to type the whole thing up at the end. By then you may find that you have forgotten much of the detail and the result will be dry, disjointed and brief. You will have a deadline to meet for the final submission and will need to keep plenty of time free to finish the writing up. A dissertation thrown together in an all-night session of writing against the clock will have all the style and elegance of a computer manual written in Chinese and then translated into English in Eastern Europe.

However, the disadvantages of doing the writing contemporaneously are that you may lack an overall style, and the parts, when put together, may not fit well. In your planning you should allow some time to reread and edit, where necessary, that which you have written.

The aim of this chapter is to help you understand what is required in the writing up of your dissertation and show you how to go about it, so that by the end of this chapter you should be able to:

- **Recognise the style required for writing up.**
- **Develop a strategy for tackling the task.**
- **Understand what is required in each chapter of the dissertation.**
- **Understand the importance of citation and referencing.**

5.1 Writing up

Read your institution's instructions for the dissertation and make sure you keep to the style that is required. Note if there is a word limit. You may be given a minimum or maximum number of words; if so, find out whether these are strict limits or just guidance. A maximum number of words is often set to make you focus on the essentials and to make your tutor's workload manageable; you write one dissertation, your tutor may have to mark many. Quantity is no substitute for quality.

5.1.1 Who are you writing for?

Think about this before you start. Who is going to read your final submission; possibly more people than you realise at the start? Identify who will be marking it. Will there just be one person or will your submission be double marked? Consider how much your tutors know about the subject and write accordingly. If you are doing a project where a tutor is not an expert in your field, you may have to give rather more detail of the basics of the theory behind your investigation. On the other hand, do not overdo the introductory material or your tutor may think that you are just trying to bulk out an otherwise rather limited investigation.

> **There are many people who may read, or at least look at, your dissertation.**

The external examiner for your course may also read parts of your dissertation. It is possible you do not know who that is or know the external examiner's area of expertise. Make sure that you write at a level that the well-educated layman can understand without making unwarranted assumptions about technical knowledge.

If your dissertation is a good one, and the chances are that it will be, given that you are taking the time to read this book in some detail, then if there are any prizes associated with your course, someone will have to make the decision about who will get them. You now have at least one more reader who may be from industry rather than an academic.

At this stage of your course you may be looking for a job for when you graduate. If so, you will want to impress your prospective employer who may be interested in the project you are doing. Alternatively, you might be hoping to go on to take a higher degree, an MSc if you are now doing a BSc or an MPhil/PhD if you are now doing an MSc. If so, your ability to undertake research will be of prime importance and the best evidence you can show will be your dissertation. It may be called for if you have an interview.

So your readership could be:

- your tutor;
- a second tutor;
- external examiner;
- prospective employers;
- MSc or PhD admissions tutor;
- your family.

5.1.2 House style

Your institution will have given you instructions for the conduct of your project and the writing of your dissertation. Those instructions may include details of the contents and the style that is required and you should follow the instructions carefully. There are three reasons for a house style. One reason is to ensure uniformity so that it will be easier to compare dissertations across the whole of your group. Another reason, which is rather more important, is to give you a structure to follow. Finally, your tutors will be gauging your ability to follow detailed instructions. However, there will be some scope for individual style so that you can show off your graphical and literary abilities.

Find out what your institution requires for the style of your dissertation and follow it.

If you have the opportunity, have a look at a few previous dissertations to get a general idea of what is expected. It is not worth spending too much time on this as some previous students may not have been too diligent in following the instructions, those instructions may have changed and you may not be looking at the best of previous students' work. Try to get your tutor to identify which the good ones are.

The house style will specify many points of detail with respect to the layout.

The opening pages will probably follow a fixed format such as:

Page 1 – Title page with a specified layout; see the example following

Page 3 – Abstract

Page 5 – Contents list

Pages 2, 4 and 6 are left blank

Page 7 – start of Chapter 1 (and the first numbered page, page 7)

Keep the title brief but informative. Four or five words are usually enough and more than twelve almost certainly unnecessary. Phrases such as 'A study of . . .' or 'An investigation into . . .' are superfluous. You should not use abbreviations in the title unless they are very well known to your entire possible readership. USA or GPS as abbreviations might be acceptable. The title indicates to the reader whether the dissertation is going to be an interesting and worthwhile read.

The title page is the first your tutor will see of your finished work. First impressions count, so make it look good.

On the title page your name should be in full, with only the family name in capitals. Other wording on the title page should be as required in your instructions. See Figure 5.1 for an example.

In the main text of the dissertation you should avoid the use of the first person singular and write it all in the third person. It is very tempting to write 'I conducted the experiment to find . . .' and 'I undertook the survey to investigate . . .' but the correct style, as in journal papers, is 'An experiment was conducted to find . . .' or if you need to indicate that it was specifically you that did the work, 'the author undertook the survey to investigate . . .'. It may all sound rather dry and dusty but that is the way professional papers are written and it is probable that you will be required to adopt that style.

KNOWLEDGE BASED ENGINEERING

IN THE DESIGN OF

INDIVIDUAL SCIENCE PROJECTS

Alison Barbara CROSS

Dissertation submitted in partial fulfilment of a
Bachelor of Science Degree in Electrical Engineering
in the School of Science and Engineering
at The University of Hometown

2008

Figure 5.1 A title page

Which of these is easier to read?

Your written work should be easy to read and it is generally better to keep your sentences short, especially if your written style is often criticised so that way the meaning will not become convoluted or obscure.	Your written work should be easy to read. Generally it is better to keep your sentences short, especially if your written style is often criticised. That way the meaning will not become convoluted or obscure.

The general rule for the use of abbreviations is that they should not appear in the title of the dissertation but may and often should be used in the text. When you first use the term, write it out in full, e.g. Global Positioning System (GPS); afterwards you just use GPS, without brackets. If you use many abbreviations it is helpful to add a glossary of terms after your contents page.

Your chapters should be subdivided with subheadings, with one or two levels. The headings will probably be in a bold style and possibly in a slightly larger font. Headings do not have a full stop at the end. Chapter headings may be centred but all other sub-headings should be justified to the left. Chapters may be numbered, as may sub-headings, especially if they are to be cross-referenced. Headings should be concise but informative. Figure 5.2 shows an example from a dissertation on 'Flood defence systems available to the homeowner'.

Each chapter should start on a new page. When you open the dissertation at any page the left page should have an even number and the right an odd number.

6

CASE STUDY – ATTENBOROUGH, NOTTINGHAMSHIRE

6.1 Trent left bank flood alleviation scheme

6.1.1 The existing environment
Before the bank was considered flooding occurred about once a . . .

6.1.2 The options considered
The options that were available were to . . .

Figure 5.2 Headings in a chapter

The style of your text may be optional. Single spacing with paragraph line breaks or a 6-point spacing before paragraphs usually looks best. It may be that you are required to increase the line spacing to 1.3, 1.5 or 2 lines.

Black should be the only colour for the text. Coloured text looks arty at best and cheap at worst and may not print well on a black and white printer.

Leave sufficient margins all around the page for binding; 20–25 mm or 0.8–1.0 inch is often used. Justification should be to the left but may be to both margins. Decide upon your formatting before you start and be consistent throughout.

Whether you use an equation editor or not is up to you. Make sure that all the symbols you use in any equations are defined in the text. It is not usually necessary to work through any calculations in full. Figure 5.3 shows an example from a project on astrogeodetic positioning. Equations, such as Equation 5.1 in Figure 5.3, should only be numbered if they are to be referred to elsewhere in the text.

A caption that is both explanatory and informative should appear with each figure and table. Many readers will only look at the abstract and the illustrations so the captions are important.

Figures and tables look best at the top or bottom of a page; when placed in the middle of a page they make the text look fragmented. A figure or table should appear at the next convenient top or bottom of a page, which should be after the paragraph where it is first mentioned. There are different ways in which figures may be numbered.

$$\lambda_A = \frac{(A_A - A_G)}{\sin \phi} + \lambda_G \qquad\qquad (5.1)$$

where

ϕ latitude

A_G and A_A geodetic and astronomical azimuth respectively

λ_G and λ_A geodetic and astronomical longitude respectively

Figure 5.3 Formula

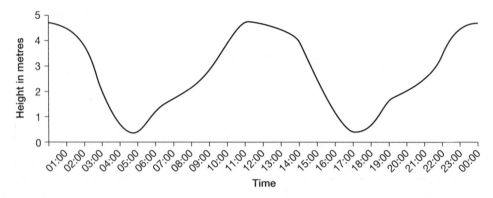

Figure 5.4 Measured tidal height at Ryde on 19 April 2007

One of the better ways is to refer to the figure by chapter and figure number in the text. For example, 'in Figure 5.4 the change in the measured height of the tide at Ryde shows that . . .' where this refers to figure number 4 in chapter 5. The figure caption appears under the figure concerned, as in Figure 5.4. The caption for a table normally appears above the table concerned.

Pictures and photographs are figures. Where possible, try to have the text where a figure or table is referred to, and the figure or table itself, appearing in the same double page spread. Each figure or table, with its caption, should be able to stand alone. The reader should not have to search the text to find out what the figure or table is all about. A reader who is skimming your dissertation may only look at the tables and figures.

5.1.3 Order of writing up

The chapters, in order within the dissertation, will probably be:

Introductory chapter

One or two literature chapters

Methodology chapter

Results chapter

Analysis of results chapter

Conclusions and recommendations chapter

This will be followed by a list of references and appendices, if any, containing data or detail that would otherwise break up the flow of the main body of the dissertation.

There is a natural order in which to write up your dissertation. Some chapters will run concurrently. You will probably start, but not finish, writing the introductory chapter and literature review chapters first. The literature review will continue through-out the project. The next chapters will follow the natural order of the project, namely the methodology, results, analysis and the conclusions and recommendations chapters. Only once everything else has been written should you write the abstract.

● 5.2 Introductory chapter

The introductory chapter is what it says; it introduces the dissertation. It is the first chapter and should contain a rationale for your investigation. This should indicate why the investigation is important and to whom, and describe the nature of the problem that needs to be addressed. State the scope of the investigation and make clear the limitations of your work.

Since your time is limited, it is likely that your investigation will be bounded by time, location and other factors. For example, it may be that you are concerned with seismic surveys for oil in a particular area of the North Sea between specific dates and the effects of that seismic activity on one particular species of whale, using data gathered by one particular organisation.

A few sentences or paragraphs stating why you chose your topic of investigation will show how motivated you are. You can amplify this by stating how you decided to go about your investigation. List briefly any past investigations into the subject. Do not go into great detail here; that will be saved for the literature review chapters.

Your introductory chapter should include a clear statement of your project's aim and objectives. It is not necessary to have specific headings of 'aim' and 'objectives' but it should be clear in the text that that is what they are. You should also state why the objectives are necessary to achieve your aim. If you have any hypotheses or key questions then this is a good place to introduce them. Again, show how they link to, and why they are important for, the investigation.

At the end of the chapter, describe the logical structure of the dissertation. You should state the chapter titles and in two or three sentences for each chapter describe their contents and indicate how one chapter follows from the previous chapter.

Finally the title of the introductory chapter should indicate the background to the problem. For example, if you are investigating the effect of seismic sonar on whales then 'Whale mortality and seismic sonar' is a better title for the first chapter than 'Introduction' which gives no information at all.

The introductory chapter should contain:

Rationale – why the investigation is important

Nature of the problem addressed

Scope of the investigation

Limitations of your work

Brief detail of past investigations

Statement of aim and objectives and why they are necessary

Hypotheses and/or key questions and why they are important

Structure of the dissertation – chapter titles and contents.

● 5.3 Literature review chapter(s)

It is most unlikely that any research is completely original and independent. All investigations follow on from work that others have done. So before you start to plan your own project it is necessary that you review and appraise what others have done before you. You will need to find and review the books and journals where their work is reported.

On the one hand, you will not want to repeat exactly what someone else has done before; there would be no originality. On the other hand, knowledge in science and engineering progresses by one person building on the work of others.

The process of evaluating the work of others in the context of the work you intend to do is called a literature review and is likely to be at least 20% of your dissertation and quite possibly as much as 40%.

5.3.1 Primary and secondary sources

Literature is considered to be either primary or secondary. Primary literature sources are those where original work is reported and include:

- academic refereed journals;
- conference proceedings;
- research theses.

They are 'primary' because they contain original peer-reviewed research work and so should reflect the latest thinking on their subjects.

The peer review process is a quality control mechanism exercised by editors of the more authoritative journals. If you write a paper and send it to such a journal then the editor will not publish it without being assured that it is of a suitable quality. The editor will send copies of your paper to a number of respected academics active in the field of study, who will give their opinions as to whether your paper meets the necessary criteria for publication in the journal, whether it could be accepted with some modifications or whether it should be rejected.

Such journals are not just for dry and dusty academics. Publications from students and young researchers like you are often welcomed. My first paper in a peer-reviewed journal was based upon a project, some years ago, undertaken at the same level as the one you are now working on.

Other primary literature sources are government publications such as those in the UK from Her Majesty's Stationery Office (HMSO). Many of these will contain statistical information.

> **When evaluating primary literature as part of your review, you will need to ask yourself how current, complete and unbiased the source is.**

Secondary literature sources include

- textbooks;
- professional journals;

■ trade journals;

■ product or software manufacturer's literature.

They are secondary in the sense that they are not written by the original researcher but someone who is compiling a document based upon the research of others. The same questions should be asked of these sources, that is, how current, complete and unbiased the source is.

It is easy to find the age of a textbook – just look for the publication date in the first few pages. Note, however, that a large or complex book may take a couple of years for an author to write after contracts have been exchanged with the publisher and that if the book is based upon an academic's teaching material, perhaps compiled over decades, some of the contents could be quite dated. Consider this book in that context. Is the material likely to date quickly or will most of it still be valid in 20 years' time?

The completeness of a book may be harder to assess as it is completeness in the context of your work that counts. If it concerns a subject you are not an expert in then compare its coverage of the topic with other books on similar subjects. Most textbooks are reasonably unbiased in that they report and describe the issues they are concerned with and usually try to give a balanced overview. When you have finished reading this book, see if you can evaluate it in the terms just described.

Professional journals are those published by professional interest groups. Those, in the UK, whose titles start with 'Royal Institution of . . .', 'Royal Society of . . .' or similar will be among the most prestigious and should have the highest levels of professional integrity. Their journals will reflect their ethics, but the journal contents will contain collections of papers and articles that reflect views of individuals within the profession. Some of the individuals may be trying to put across their own specific points of view and therefore you will need to consider questions of bias more closely.

Trade journals are written to inform and promote the interest groups they represent. By their very nature they will be generally upbeat upon the subjects they cover and are unlikely to present the activities of their sponsors or advertisers in a negative light. You will need to be diligent in guarding against bias.

> **Manufacturers' literature is probably the least unbiased of all.**

The purpose of a manufacturer's literature is to present the manufacturer's equipment, product or software in the most favourable light. It is unlikely that there will be any untrue statements if the manufacturer has a reputation it wishes to retain, but the facts that are given will be selective and there will seldom be any objective comparison with similar products from other manufacturers.

If you are going to use a manufacturer's literature as a reference it is advisable to report only the technical facts of the product, but be very wary of being drawn by the manufacturer's opinion of its own product. Statements like 'this product is ideal for . . .' are seldom true. One problem that occurs with such literature is that of trying to date it. Manufacturers do not like their products to appear dated and so will often not date their literature. You can sometimes track down a publication date by looking at the printer's reference, if there is one, on the back page.

5.3.2 The internet

The internet is an extensive and ever-changing source of primary and secondary information. It is also a source of some of the most appalling rubbish. Unlike the primary and secondary sources described above, it is more difficult to separate the gems from the dross.

Much that appears in books and journals also appears on the internet, including some learned papers. However, there are also some papers that appear learned but have not been through a peer review process. When referring to internet sources your biggest problem will be to assess the quality of what you have found. One way of making that assessment is to ask the following questions.

> For internet sources ask:
>
> how current?
>
> how correct?
>
> how complete?
>
> how unbiased?
>
> who put it there and why.
>
> Look for any evidence of QA/peer review.

As an exercise, and using the questions above, see how you rate the website of the Institute of Biology at www.iob.org and compare it with the website of the Flat Earth Society at www.theflatearthsociety.org.

5.3.3 Finding references

By now you will have found your institution's library. A library used to be just a place where books were kept but today there are many more sources of information available. Books are the most obvious source and you will be able to use the online catalogue to help find suitable books. The catalogue will probably also be available off campus and you will be able to search by subject or author. Your library will also have back numbers of journals, conference proceedings and theses, although the latter may be limited to MPhil and PhD only.

Finding what you want in journals can be tricky because there are so many journals on such a wide variety of subjects. Scanning the shelves to find the journals that cater for your interests is a good way to identify the journals that publish in your area of interest but not a good way to find the papers on the specific issues that interest you.

Use the library's electronic search capability to find databases and journals. You will be able to browse in different ways such as A–Z lists of journals or use catalogues to look through collections of applicable databases.

You may be able to do 'metasearches' of many electronic resources as well as the library catalogue. You should be able to link to abstracts of papers and for some you will also be able to find the full-text versions depending upon which databases your library subscribes to. You will probably need an 'Athens' username and password to access these databases. Your library will be able to tell you how to get yours. Box 5.1 lists some useful databases.

Box 5.1 Useful databases

Some useful databases to look out for:

ANTE (Abstracts in New Technology and Engineering)

ASCE (American Society of Civil Engineers)

Barbour (Engineering regulations and suppliers)

British Standards

Building Cost Information Service

Building Law Reports Database

Business Source Premier Database

CAB Abstracts (agriculture, animal health, conservation, forestry, human health, human nutrition)

Compendex (interdisciplinary engineering database)

Construction and Building Abstracts

Digimap Ordnance Survey Data Collection

ENDS Report (environmental information)

Environment Abstracts (impact of technology on the environment)

Environmental Management (environmental legislation and guidelines)

FORS (Forensic Science Service)

Geological Society Index

IBSEDEX (for mechanical and electrical services in buildings)

ICEA (International Civil Engineering Abstracts)

ICONDA (International Construction Database)

Index to Theses (doctoral and master degrees of UK and Irish Universities)

INSPEC (physics and engineering)

Institute of Physics online journals

ISI Proceedings (science and technology)

Key Skill: Animal Anatomy and Physiology Collection

Knovel (aerospace, biochemistry, chemistry, electronics, engineering, environment, food, pharmaceuticals, safety, textiles)

Land, Life and Leisure (agriculture, conservation, environmental, equine, estate management, forestry, horticulture, organic husbandry, recreation, rural planning, tourism)

LexisNexis Executive (news and business intelligence)

NTIS (National Technical Information Service – US government-funded scientific, technical, engineering topics)

Ornamental Plants Plus

Polymer Library Database

PubMed (biomedical literature)

RAM (Recent Advances in Manufacturing)

SAE Technical Papers Database (automotive engineering)

Science Citation Index

Science Direct

SciFinder Scholar (chemical)

SGI-Line (Swedish Geotechnical Institute Database)

Westlaw (law reports and law journals)

WildPro (captive and free-ranging wild animals)

Zetoc (engineering, medicine, science, technology)

5.3.4 Reviewing references

So now you have found some useful and relevant references in your institution's library and on the internet; what do you do next? A pile of references is just a disordered pile of paper; you need to extract the information that is going to be useful to you. The best way to do this is by taking notes. With each potential reference, consider what you know already and hence what you need to get from this reference. Consider also what makes this reference different from the others that you have come across. You might make the notes on paper but better would be to create a computer file. For each reference identify the following:

The Author(s)

Year of publication

Title of the paper, article, book and chapter if it is in an edited book

Volume and issue number for journals

Publisher and place of publication

Page numbers in the journal, or chapter number in an edited book

Your library classification number and where it is in the library

Web page URL and the date you last accessed it

The URL or uniform resource locator is the web page address and often starts with http://www.

You will need all this information for two reasons. One is so that you can find the reference again if you need to, and the other is because you will need this data for your reference list; more about that below.

Having got these details, now extract the information that you will need to refer to. You will probably want to make notes about the main issues and arguments raised and the conclusions that the author has drawn. You may also need some details of the author's methodology.

Identify and use only the information that is directly related to your project. It is too easy to be swamped with unnecessary data.

When you make your notes do not just copy sections of the reference into your own computer. There are two reasons: one is that you will need to write up any material in your own words for your dissertation and the other is that you will be in grave danger of inadvertent plagiarism. If you copy some text from another source, e.g. 'copy and paste' from the internet, and much later use the file to 'copy and paste' into your final document then you will be including text which is not your own. There are severe penalties for plagiarism, inadvertent or deliberate, which is why there is a whole chapter on the subject in this book. Beware!

5.3.5 Critical appraisal of your literature

The critical appraisal is the most important part of your literature review. There is very little merit in merely identifying other people's ideas and words. It is what *you* do with it that counts. You will need to look for agreement and contradiction between other authors as well as looking for recurrent ideas and issues. Look for any analysis or critical appraisal by others.

Remember that a literature review is about *critically appraising* the literature associated with a subject, not just about extracting information from the literature and repeating it in your submission. Your literature review should critically appraise the literature associated with your project.

In considering each section and each statement, ask yourself the question 'so what?' to help you tease out meaning, ideas and evaluation. This is one of the most difficult parts of the dissertation but also the one where you can add most value to your own work, by evaluation, i.e. critical appraisal, of others.

Present all your work in an orderly and logical progression. Break your literature review up into sections by subject and deal with each separately. The literature review should:

- briefly introduce the subject;
- state the arguments from the references;
- give **your** critical appraisal of those arguments (the most important part);
- list the references (in the reference list at the end of the dissertation).

Box 5.2 shows an example from a project concerned with survey where one objective was 'To identify methods for classifying survey control'.

● 5.4 Citing references

Citing references is concerned with acknowledging the work of others. The citation is the indicator in your text that refers to the full reference which is in the list at the end of the dissertation.

Correct citation allows you to demonstrate that you have reviewed the existing knowledge on which your work is based. Others who are interested can then find and follow up your references easily. If you do not do this then it may appear that you are presenting the work of others as your own. If so, you would be guilty of plagiarism and

Box 5.2 A short critical appraisal

The title	**Methods for Classifying Survey Control**
The introduction	Survey control points form an essential framework for subsequent survey work of lower accuracy. To assess the quality of the latter work it is necessary to know the quality of the initial control.
The arguments	USACE (1994) classify survey control in the traditional manner by referring to orders of control defined by 'Point Closure Ratios'. The classification of a control point is defined by the misclosure in the survey, such as a traverse, in which the control point lies. In subsequent surveys it is assumed that the coordinates of the point are fixed and that uncertainty in the coordinates is not transferred to any detail survey points from the existing control point.
	Johnson (2004), like most modern textbooks, makes little mention of orders of control but describes survey precision in more statistical terms. The precision of control points is in terms of 'error ellipses' which are figures of uncertainty. The precision of any detail point surveyed using one of these control points will also be expressed by an 'error ellipse'. It will reflect the uncertainty of the control point and the quality of the detail survey observations.
	Schofield (2001) remains silent on the subject and contents himself with describing survey methods for establishing control and propagation of error as quite distinct subjects and does not relate the latter to the former.
The critical appraisal	The USACE (1994) approach takes no account of the way error can propagate through a survey and assumes that the precision of a control point can be defined by the misclosure in a simple network. Such an approach is simplistic in that it can only use specific survey figures where compensating errors in the observations may disguise the true errors in the control points.
	By contrast, Johnson (2004) makes use of all the available statistical survey data and approaches the problem of deriving imperfect coordinates from imperfect observations with a fully rigorous statistical process. Therefore individual figures of uncertainty may be ascribed to all the control points in a survey, blunders in observations detected and removed, and actual, as opposed to assumed, precision of the survey observations found. Therefore this is by far the better method but has the drawback that the computational process is much more complex and in practice requires appropriate software.
	Schofield (2001) is entirely lacking on this subject and the author will need to consider how this subject should be treated in the next edition. Greater discussion on the nature of uncertainty in survey control would significantly improve this book.*
From the references list at the end of the dissertation	Johnson, A., 2004. Plane and Geodetic Surveying. Abingdon: Spon Press.
	Schofield, W., 2001. Engineering Surveying. 5th edn. Oxford: Butterworth Heinemann.
	USACE, 1994. Topographic Survey Control. [online]. US Army Corps of Engineers. Available at URL: <http://www.usace.army.mil/publications/eng-manuals/em1110-1-1005/c-3.pdf> [accessed 28 December 2006].

* It does – see the 6th edition by Schofield and Breach

so will be guilty of a serious breach of the rules by which your work is judged. The penalties for plagiarism are likely to be as severe as those for being caught cheating in an examination. Therefore it is important to get your citations and referencing correct.

You may have noticed, in the entire book up to this stage, that almost all guidance has been prefaced with the word 'should' rather than 'must'. If there is one occasion where that latter word needs to be used, it is here.

> **Each time you use the work of others it <u>MUST</u> be properly referenced.**

If this all sounds a bit heavy handed or threatening so far, do not be concerned. Referencing is easily done if you follow the rules. There are two systems in current use, the Harvard and the numerical systems. Generally the Harvard system is preferred and that system will briefly be described here. You may find that there is a full guide on your institution's web pages, possibly those associated with the library.

5.4.1 The citation

Citing in the Harvard system is very easy because all that is required are the author's name and date of publication. Look back to the critical appraisal above and in the text you will see the words 'Johnson (2004)'; this is the citation. At the end of the example there was a short reference list and one of the references was:

> Johnson, A., 2004. Plane and Geodetic Surveying. Abingdon: Spon Press.

Notice in the citation that only the surname followed by date in brackets is required. An alternative form of citation, in slightly changed text, would be: 'The precision of control points may be in terms of "error ellipses" (Johnson 2004).' Here both name and date are in the brackets and the citation is not a grammatically necessary part of the sentence.

If there is more than one Johnson citation of 2004 then they would be written as Johnson (2004a), Johnson (2004b) etc. If you use a quotation the page number should be included, for example Johnson (2004, p 99). An example of how to use a direct quotation is given in Section 8.1.

5.4.2 The reference

The reference can be a little more complicated because there are many more possibilities. In essence the reference should provide all the information for the interested reader to be able to track down the reference. The necessary detail for a book is:

Author, Year. Title. Edition. Place: Publisher.

The title may be written in bold type or italics to make it stand out. If there is only one author such as in Johnson (2004), then the reference is as in the last section. If there are two or three authors they are in the order as listed on the title page and the form is:

> Adds, J., Larkcom, E., and Miller, R., 2003. Respiration and co-ordination. Cheltenham: Nelson Thornes Ltd.

With four or more authors the form is:

> Landau, L., et al., 1995. Mechanics. Oxford: Butterworth-Heinemann Ltd.

If the book has been edited:

> Colbeck, I., ed. 2007. Environmental chemistry of aerosols. Oxford: Blackwell.

A corporate author:

> English Heritage, 2006. Hazardous history. Swindon: English Heritage.

For a conference paper the second part is the person(s) or organisation that edits the proceedings, for example:

> Barthelmes, F., Dietrich, R., 1991. Use of point masses on optimized positions for the approximation of the gravity field. In: Rapp, R. ed. IAG Symposium 106, Determination of the geoid present and future. Milan, Italy, June 11–13, 1990. London: Springer-Verlag, pp 484–493.

Theses and student dissertations:

> Ahmed, S., 2005. The threat of a rising sea level to Bangladesh. MSc dissertation, Nottingham Trent University.

If no author can be traced:

> Anon., 2005. Watch and clock escapements. Gloucester: Dodo Press.

If the publisher details are missing, replace the details with (s.l.): (s.n.). This stands for 'sine loco' and 'sine nominee' and they mean that the place and name are unknown. For example, the last reference would appear as:

> Anon., 2005. Watch and clock escapements. (s.l.): (s.n.).

The place of publication is not so important, but you should try to find the name of the publisher at least. Journal article references are in the form:

Author, Year. Article title. Journal title, Volume, Pages. Place: Publisher.

> Yang, Z., Chen, Y., 2001. Determination of Hong Kong gravimetric geoid. Survey Review, Vol. 36 No. 279, pp 23–34. London: Commonwealth Association of Surveying and Land Economy (CASTLE).

The style for web pages is a little different. The format is:

Author, Year. Title [online]. Place: Publisher. Available at: <URL> [Accessed Date].

The author and year may be a bit tricky to determine from the information available on the page, in which case use the organisation associated with the page and the current year. For example:

> US Government, 2007. The official US time. [online]. National Institute of Standards and Technology (NIST) and US Naval Observatory (USNO). Available at: <URL:http://www.time.gov/> [Accessed 4 January 2007].

Electronic journal articles are referenced in a similar way.

A personal email should appear as:

Author, (email from address) year. Email title, Day and month. Email to: recipient (address). For example:

> Jones, J. (john.jones@ntu.ac.uk), 2007. Biochemical integrity, 28 February. Email to: Stella Smith (stella.smith@ntu.ac.uk).

This is not an exhaustive list but it covers most document types you are likely to use. Consult your own institution's guide for more details.

5.5 Methodology chapter

The methodology chapter is where you write about how you conducted the research. This chapter should follow logically from the literature review chapter(s). You should describe or list the data you have identified that you need, and say why you need them.

Different types of data, qualitative and quantitative, and their methods of analysis have already been covered in Chapters 3 and 4.

Say what the potential sources of data were, and from those, the sources that you selected. State why you selected those sources and why you rejected the others. Having identified the data you had intended to collect, now say how you intended to analyse the data once you had it. So far, this is all information that you had at the planning stage and therefore this part could be written up, at least in draft form, before you start work.

> **Next describe the data you actually did collect and your method of doing so.**

As almost nothing in this life actually goes entirely to plan, there will be changes from your expectations. This is perfectly normal and does not reflect upon your competence whatsoever; indeed if the work went perfectly to plan then it might suggest that you had taken on only a trivial task. What goes wrong is often more interesting than what goes right.

There will be problems that you will have to face up to and deal with, so write them up as they will show your tutor how you have been personally involved in the project. On the other hand, do not use this section to list a catalogue of woes as an excuse for failing to achieve anything; that won't impress your tutor at all.

Describe how you got your results from your data and the method by which you analysed those results. If you used quantitative methods then state the statistical processes that you used.

If you used questionnaires or interviews, describe your thinking behind their design and structure. If your method involved creating some original mathematical derivations then these should be shown. Likewise, if you had to devise a non-standard or novel piece of equipment then describe it here. These show strong originality on your part and are likely to score heavily in your final marks.

You could also state what other methods you would have used had you been able to do so.

● 5.6 Results chapter

The results chapter should present the results that you achieved in a clear and factual way. This chapter should flow logically from the previous chapter on the methodology. Be careful to keep the contents of the two chapters separate: the previous one is about how you did the work; this one is about what you achieved from it.

> **The results chapter should contain a detailed summary of your results so you should extract the important results and present them in an easy-to-read form.**

If you have used interviews or questionnaires then it is likely that you will need to summarise the data by grouping results. Consider carefully how this should be done as you will be referring to these grouped results in your analysis.

If you have numerical results then they may be presented in a table or as a graph. If the individual numbers in your results are important then a table might be better but if you are more interested in trends or change, that will probably be easier to see in a graph. Consider the presentation, in Table 5.1 and Figure 5.5, of the same results and judge for yourself which gives the more immediate and clear impression of the rate of growth of a leaf. The results show how the average length of a sample of leaves changes over time.

It is hard to see from the table what is happening to the leaf samples, other than that they get longer with time. The graph, however, shows that the growth rate is virtually static at the beginning and end of the period but at a maximum at the middle.

Table 5.1 Leaf growth

Time since start days	Leaf length millimetres
0	50.28
7	50.23
14	50.86
21	54.18
28	57.78
35	64.23
42	72.82
49	80.70
56	90.01
63	107.71
70	116.00
77	123.20
84	133.03
91	139.08
98	143.57
105	146.37
112	149.15
119	149.13

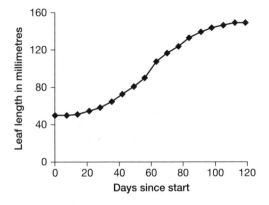

Figure 5.5 Leaf growth

If you have lots of numerical data then presenting them within the chapter may break up the flow of what you are saying. It would therefore be better to present this level of detail in an appendix. Appendices come after the chapters and reference list. If you do use one or more appendices they must be referred to somewhere in the chapters.

● 5.7 Analysis chapter

Just as the results chapter is quite separate from the methodology chapter, the analysis chapter would normally also be separate from the results chapter. This is the chapter where you draw meaning from your results and so will be applying statistical techniques to them. There are some details in Chapter 4.

Start with a paragraph or two describing the scope of the chapter; what the chapter is going to be about. Any statistical analysis here may include details of significance of results and statistical correlation between results, even if the original data were qualitative.

Include a descriptive as well as a numerical analysis of the results.

For all the statistical analysis that may take place, here you will need to include a descriptive analysis of the results. A statistic is just a number, and as a number, is usually meaningless. What is required here is a descriptive interpretation. Tell your reader what the numbers really mean and why the results and their analysis are important. This is another part of your dissertation where you can demonstrate your understanding and originality.

If you have a hypothesis your analysis should lead you to accept the hypothesis or reject it in favour of the alternative hypothesis. You should now also be in a position to answer any key questions that you formally posed in your project proposal.

● 5.8 Conclusions and recommendations chapter

There are two distinct parts to this chapter, the conclusions and the recommendations. Remember that conclusions conclude, so you should not be introducing any new material here. Reflect upon the original project aim and if, how and why it has been modified since you started. Review your research objectives and consider any modifications you have made to them in a similar way. If you had a hypothesis or key questions consider any changes you made to them. If there have been no changes, say so.

Now state why you have accepted your hypothesis or the alternative hypothesis and comment on the strength of that acceptance. Next, consider each of your objectives and reflect upon how well, or otherwise, they have been achieved. This will naturally lead you to review your aim, and again you can consider how well that was achieved.

Do not worry that all your conclusions are not positive.

Do not try to make things look better than they are; if your conclusions are not backed up by your analysis, your analysis by your results, and your results by your data, you will lose marks for trying to pull the wool over the eyes of your tutor. On the other hand, if you present a clear and unbiased view of what you have and have not achieved you will get much more credit for being objective and self-critical. Self-criticism should not be apologetic or disparaging but exploratory and insightful.

At this stage you can also reflect upon the strengths and the limitations of what you have achieved. It is more than likely that you have not achieved all that you hoped for at the outset. You may also now, with hindsight, consider any flaws in your methodology that made this so.

All this will then lead you into the very last part of the main text of your dissertation where you should consider where the project could go next, either by yourself if you were to continue the research, or by others if they were to develop the ideas you have researched. The project has now come full circle in the sense that in Chapter 1 of this book the statement 'whatever you do, it will build on the work of others' was used to indicate that you will start by reviewing literature. Now others may include reviewing your dissertation at the start of their research.

 ## 5.9 Abstract

The abstract is the last piece of formal writing that you do. It is the last because, although it goes at the front of your dissertation, you will need to draw upon the whole of your work to write it.

The abstract would normally be about 200–250 words. Check your own institution's requirements as this may vary from institution to institution. You will need to make several attempts at a draft before you have a final polished version of the abstract. It is important to get this right because it will be the first part of the dissertation that your tutor will read, and first impressions count.

> **Your abstract should encapsulate the essence of your dissertation and you will find it a challenge to get that into the necessary few words.**

The abstract usually starts with the word 'Abstract' followed by formal details of author, year, title, course and institution. The text then has five parts: information about the topic under investigation, including a statement about the problem being investigated, the method that was used, a very brief summary of the main results, the major conclusions and a short list of key words. All this should fit onto one side of a piece of paper. Before you start you should check to see if your institution requires something slightly different.

Boxes 5.3a–e show some examples; headings have been added to the left-hand side to help identify the component parts. These would not, of course, appear in your abstract.

Box 5.3a Abstract – Newtonian Dynamics

Abstract

WILLMER, D., 2007. A Computational Investigation into Newtonian and Modified Newtonian Dynamics at solar system and galactic levels. BSc Astrophysics dissertation. School of Biomedical and Natural Sciences. Nottingham Trent University.

Information about topic	It is assumed that the laws of gravity are fairly well known – in fact, this is not the case. The concept of 'dark matter' was invented in order to explain the gravitational anomalies we see when we look at movements within galaxies; however, dark matter cannot explain everything. It could be that a physical equation as widely accepted as Newton's Law of Gravity needs revising in order to agree with the observational data currently available.
Method used	A program was written using Newtonian physics to model the dynamical behaviour of the solar system as far as Neptune. Various algorithms for solving differential equations were implemented to test for the best candidate. A program was written to give the Cartesian coordinates of the planets at a user-defined date. The solar system was then modelled for a chosen time and the results compared with NASA data. Gravity was then investigated computationally on galactic and solar levels in an attempt to show whether a Modified Dynamics theory, such as Milgrom's MOND, or the Dark Matter theory gives a better model for the observed data in the context of the 'mass discrepancy' problem.
Main results	It was found that MOND provides a closer fit to observed data.
Major conclusions	It is proposed that MOND effects can be witnessed in the inner solar system.
Keywords	Keywords: gravity, computational modelling, MOND, galaxies.

Box 5.3b Abstract – Numerical Analysis

Abstract

CHARAVANAMUTTU, S., 2007. Numerical Back Analysis of a Steep Slope Landfill Lining System. MSc Geotechnical Engineering dissertation. School of Architecture Design and the Built Environment, Nottingham Trent University.

Information about topic	Steep slope landfill liners are constructed in deep quarries using mineral liners which rely on the lateral support provided by Municipal Solid Waste (MSW) for overall stability. Recent monitoring of a steep wall liner in Nottingham indicated that poor compaction of the waste placed against it had caused the failure of the seal by an overturning mode.

Method used	The finite element method was used to analyse the steep slope liner. Limited geotechnical data were available for the elements of the steep slope liner and the MSW. Therefore the steep slope liner was back analysed using published geotechnical parameters for the MSW and interpolated parameters for the other elements of the liner. The finite element analyses were undertaken using PLAXIS code. The MSW was modelled using both Mohr–Coulomb and a more advanced constitutive model, the Soft Soil Creep model, which allows for the effect of creep in the waste.
Main results	The interface stress calculated and the settlements of the liner and the MSW were compared with measurements taken. The calculated stresses and settlements were found to be comparable within 40% of the observed values.
Major conclusions	The Soft Soil Creep model can be used to model MSW.
Keywords	Keywords: municipal solid waste, back analysis, steep slope liner, finite element, PLAXIS.

Box 5.3c Abstract – Engineer and Architect

Abstract

BREALEY, A. 2006. The structural engineer/architect relationship. MSc Structural Renovation dissertation. School of the Built Environment, Nottingham Trent University.

Information about topic	The architect/engineer relationship is a complicated one. How well the relationship works affects the difficulties that will arise with the design of a particular project. Historically, architects and engineers had a common ancestor in the master builder, but the disciplines were split during the industrial revolution. Typically each discipline attracted a different personality type and so misunderstandings and jealousies between the two disciplines began when they had to work together. Other factors that affect the relationship today include the competency and experience of the architects and engineers, client, budget, and timescale of the project.
Method used	A questionnaire enquiring about the relationship was sent to fifty engineering and fifty architectural small businesses in the Midlands.
Main results	Architects and engineers only experienced conflicts with the other some of the time or rarely. Most agree that the relationship could be improved by bringing architects and engineers together at undergraduate level for collaboration on joint projects, teaching each group of students about the other's subject and explaining the duties and responsibilities of each.
Major conclusions	However, the effectiveness of the architect/engineer relationship will always come down to personalities and compatibility. When an architect/engineer pairing has worked well then the pair will often choose to work together again on future projects.
Keywords	Keywords: architect, engineer, interrelationship.

Box 5.3d Abstract – Flood Storage

Abstract

JACKSON. C, 2007. Use of glacial till in Flood Storage Embankments. MSc Geotechnical Engineering dissertation. School of Architecture Design and the Built Environment, Nottingham Trent University.

Information about topic	Flooding has already become a significant hazard in northern parts of the UK. It is here that the thickest deposits of glacial till are encountered. In current literature information about Flood Storage Embankments is limited. Because of flooding in the town of Northallerton and surrounding villages in 2000 and 2002 the local authority decided to investigate the feasibility of installation of a comprehensive flood defence scheme around the affected locations.
Method used	A ground investigation using a combination of cable percussive, rotary coring and machine excavated trial pits was undertaken, followed by a range of geotechnical laboratory tests.
Main results	Analysis of this data showed that the glacial till in the Northallerton area was suitable in the most part for use in constructing the embankments and also as a foundation material for the Flood Storage Embankments.
Major conclusions	Review of the data with other authors' work on glacial till showed a reasonable correlation; however, differences were also noted, and as a result of the small sample size it is deemed unreasonable to make the assumption that all glacial till material would be suitable for such construction projects.
Keywords	Keywords: flood storage embankment, foundations, glacial till, suitability.

Box 5.3e Abstract – Correction of Digital Images

Abstract

VAJZOVIC, T., 2006. Dust Removal and Colour Correction in Digital Images of Slide-Based Works of Art. BSc Computational Physics dissertation. School of Biomedical and Natural Sciences. Nottingham Trent University.

Information about topic	Tate Modern's large collection of slide-projected works of art are damaged by use. In order to preserve them Tate Modern wish to store digital representations of the images.
Method used	Software was developed to remove dust from digital images of slide-based works of art and to convert them to a documented absolute colour space. Dust was removed by accurate alignment of repeat scans of the same transparency and the application of a median image operation. Alignment was found by statistical analysis of the correlation coefficient of many small areas of the images. Linearisation functions and a colour transformation matrix were found by analysis of an image of a Kodak Q-60 Colour Input Target combined with published data for the batch of the target.

Main results	Linearisation functions can be used to obtain linear intensity response values from the scanner's RGB sensors. The transform matrix converts the scanner's RGB stimulus sensitivities into XYZ tristimulus coordinates for the CIE 2° standard observer and from the scanner's light source to the D50 standard illuminant.
Major conclusions	The final image can be stored as tristimulus values using the VIPS or TIFF file format.
Keywords	Keywords: Tate, digital image, colour transformation, linearization.

● 5.10 Tops and tails

Now you are almost finished, but there are still a few more pages to do before you can hand in the dissertation.

After the title page and abstract comes the contents list. The contents list includes the chapter headings with sub-headings, appendices and any enclosed items. The contents list should provide the reader with an indication of the extent of the dissertation. The contents should be on one page only. You will write it last when you know all the chapters and their sections and their page numbers.

Optionally, after the contents list you may have a glossary of terms, frontispiece, and an acknowledgements page. Some institutions may also require that you have a list of tables and a list of figures.

A glossary of terms (Figure 5.6) in alphabetical order is useful if you have used many abbreviations in your text. The reader who is unfamiliar with them can then decode them easily without having to find the first usage of each one. The glossary is additional to the definitions of the abbreviations at their first usage in the text.

	Glossary of Terms
AHD	Australian Height Datum
CID	charge injection device
DEM	digital elevation model
DoD	United States Department of Defense
GPS	Global Positioning System
ODN	Ordnance Datum Newlyn
TRF	Terrestrial Reference Frame
WGS84	World Geodetic System 1984
...	...

Figure 5.6 A glossary of terms

> I haven't a clue as to how my story will end. But that's all right.
> When you set out on a journey and night covers the road, you
> don't conclude that the road has vanished. And how else could
> we discover the stars?
>
> Anon

Figure 5.7 A frontispiece

A frontispiece may be a pertinent photograph that you took, or piece of your own original artwork that brings out or illustrates a major aspect of the project. It may just be a witty quotation that touches on an aspect of your project. If your dissertation has very few illustrations, here is a chance to help bring it to life for the casual reader. See Figure 5.7.

Views upon whether acknowledgements are appropriate are mixed. You may feel the need to acknowledge your boyfriend's support while you were immersed in the project or your wife who kept your firstborn out of earshot while you struggled with the paperwork, but such text is unlikely to impress your tutor.

You should, however, acknowledge substantial support you have received from anyone who did so beyond the call of duty, for example an organisation or employer that gave money or equipment or a person who gave you their time. Your tutor might be flattered by your recognition or may be nauseated by blatant sycophancy; you will have to judge that one for yourself. Have a look at the acknowledgements page (at the beginning) of this book.

A list of figures (Figure 5.8) helps the reader find a particular figure from the description in the caption.

Likewise, a list of tables (Figure 5.9) may be useful if there are a significant number in the text. The list will include the caption and table number.

After the last chapter comes the reference list. Do not call it a chapter because it is not one. The reference list must be in alphabetical order. This is easily achieved in Microsoft Word. Simply block the unsorted list of references. Under 'Table' select 'Sort' then sort by 'paragraphs' with the type as 'text' and 'ascending'. See Figure 5.10.

List of Figures	Page
1.1 Orthometric and ellipsoidal height	2
2.1 Relationship between geoid and ellipsoid	8
2.2 A geoid model for Portsmouth	28
3.1 Two Position Circles	42
3.2 Plotting a Position Line	44
3.3 Position Line solution	46
... ...	...

Figure 5.8 A list of figures

List of Tables

Figure 5.9 A list of tables

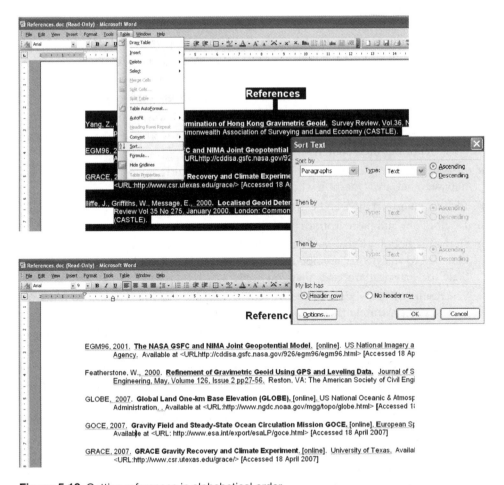

Figure 5.10 Getting references in alphabetical order

Finally there are the appendices where you will have put any quantities of data, calculation summaries, sub-documents such as blank questionnaires and other blocks of information that would have broken up the flow of the narrative.

Having compiled all the paperwork, you should check your institution's instructions with respect to the binding and submission requirements.

5.11 Summary

■ Write up your dissertation as you go along.

■ Plan for time to reread and edit what you have written.

■ Think about who you are writing for.

■ Find out about and conform to your institution's house style for writing up.

■ Keep your written style simple.

■ Check your institution's requirements for headings, pagination, line spacing, text colour, acceptable fonts and size, equation style, margins, figure and table captions.

■ The usual order of writing up is introductory, literature review, methodology, results, analysis, conclusions and recommendations chapters and abstract.

■ The introductory chapter should contain a rationale for and scope of your investigation with the problem to be addressed, its aim and objectives.

■ The literature review chapter recognises and evaluates the work of others.

■ Use the correct form for citations in the text and references in the reference list.

■ The literature review is about critically appraising the works of others, not simply about reporting their contents.

■ Be wary of internet sources. Try to determine how current, correct, complete, and unbiased they are. Question who put the material there and why.

■ Identify your references and extract the important information and reference details.

■ Do not copy and paste from the internet into your notes.

■ In the methodology chapter describe the data you intended to collect and how you intended to analyse it. Describe the data you actually collected and how you did so. State the statistical processes that you used.

■ The results chapter should contain a detailed summary of your results. Consider the best way of presenting them; consider using tables and graphs.

■ In the analysis chapter you draw meaning from your results, probably using statistical techniques.

■ Include details of significance of results and statistical correlation between results but also a descriptive interpretation. What do the numbers really mean? Why are the results and their analysis important?

■ If you have a hypothesis, state whether you accept it or the alternative hypothesis.

■ In the conclusions and recommendations chapter refer back to the original project aim and objectives. Conclusions may not all be positive. Present a clear and unbiased view of what you have and have not achieved and the limitations of your work. Do not introduce new material. Describe how the project could be developed further.

■ Take care to get the abstract right. 'Abstract' is the heading followed by author, title, course and institution details. Follow with information about the topic, method, summary of results, conclusions and key words; all on one side of a piece of paper.

■ Compile a contents list.

■ Consider the need for a glossary of terms, frontispiece, acknowledgements page, lists of tables and figures.

What next?

That depends at what stage you have got to.

If you are at the planning stage, use the ideas in this chapter to help you to decide how to proceed.

If you are part way through your project, refer to the appropriate part of this chapter for ideas on how to write that section.

If you are almost at the end of the write-up reread this chapter to make sure you have not left anything important out.

Allow plenty of time for the write-up. You cannot deliver a first-class dissertation in a rush.

Tips and hints

A little forethought can save a lot of time and many tears.

This chapter is to help you avoid the pitfalls awaiting the unwary; life's Pooh traps for Heffalumps (with apologies to A.A. Milne, author of *Winnie the Pooh*). By identifying what can go wrong it may be possible to be prepared and so avoid mistakes. Even when disaster strikes it may still be possible to salvage enough from the wreckage still to make a respectable submission. But best of all is to take action right from the start to make disaster much less likely.

The aim of this chapter is to present some ideas and strategies that will aid you while conducting your project and writing up your dissertation. By the end of this chapter you should be able to:

- **Recognise what can go wrong with the project and dissertation.**
- **Recover from disaster.**
- **Develop strategies for avoiding difficulties.**

6.1 What can go wrong?

There are several things that can go wrong. Here are some of the more common ones.

6.1.1 Inertia

The most common thing that does go wrong is failing to make a start.

Some students are intimidated by the nature, scope and size of the job before them. They go into a sort of state of shock at the apparently overwhelming task and put off making a start in favour of more immediate deadlines, or sometimes they do nothing at all.

So what is needed here is the recognition that it is a big task, but like any big task, it can be broken down into its component parts which can then be sized and put into a logical order. This is what planning is about, breaking an unmanageably large task into a series of manageable smaller ones, so that each small task can be achieved, ticked off and put aside. When all the smaller tasks are complete, the whole dissertation is complete as well. Job done!

> **Do not be intimidated; it is a big task, but manageable.**

6.1.2 Topic too broad

If your topic is too broad then you will soon find that your workload is not going to be achievable in the time that you have available. To avoid this happening, give serious thought to the question that your aim seeks to answer. Similarly, do not take on too many objectives in support of the aim.

If you find at this stage that the project is looking like it will be too large then return to your question and narrow it down some more to reduce the scope of the project to that which is manageable. This can be difficult at the beginning of a project, especially as you may not have done anything like a project before. If you are going to err at this stage it is better to err on the side of having too narrow a project than one that is too broad.

> **A project that is rather narrow is less likely to give problems than one that is too broad.**

It may be that you are well into your project when you realise that it is going to be impossible to complete it as planned. In that case, examine each of your objectives and see if any can be abandoned without seriously compromising the integrity of the whole project.

Alternatively, consider if any experiments or programmes of field data capture can be reduced in scope. Can you reduce the number of questions on your questionnaire or the number of questionnaires you propose to send out? Can the analysis be simplified? If you do any of these things, will that affect your objectives or the aim? If so, can you redefine the aim to accommodate these?

Consider these options and then talk with your tutor. You will get a lot more sympathy if you recognise the difficulties and review the options. It will show that you can plan and respond to changing conditions and you may even get a few marks for this. You are much more likely to have your tutor on your side if you are making realistic and positive attempts to cope with an unforeseen problem than if you turn up at your tutor's door two weeks before the hand-in deadline saying 'I've got a problem; tell me what to do'.

6.1.3 Too little time to collect and analyse data

The reason for not having enough time to collect and analyse the data is probably bad planning. One part of the project proposal is concerned with identifying what data are to be collected, how that is to be done, and what is to be done with the data once you have got them.

However, in spite of the best of planning, your programme may not have worked out as you anticipated. If you find that you are running out of time at the data collection stage you will have little option but to cut short some of the data collection and work with what you have. This may not be ideal, but as time is finite and inflexible, you have little choice.

> **You may need to be ruthless with yourself.**

If you have got to the stage where you have all the data but the analysis is going badly, then similar ideas apply. Consider whether abandoning some of your data will ease the problem. This may be hard to do as it will mean that previous time and effort are being thrown away. Alternatively, consider if it is possible to conduct a simpler, but less sophisticated analysis to save time. This may limit the conclusions that you can draw but it will give you something more you can add to your recommendations for further study.

6.1.4 Failure to get data

If a campaign of fieldwork or an experiment has been planned, then usually the data can be obtained. It may be that the data are not of the expected quality; in which case the conclusions that can be drawn from the analysis of the results are limited. Failure to get sufficient data, or even data at all, is more likely to occur with questionnaires. If the questionnaires are badly composed and sent out late to an inappropriate target group then the disaster may not be apparent until well into the project.

To counter this, follow the guidance in Sections 3.8–3.10. Test your questionnaires with a pilot study to gauge the likely rate of return early on so that you have time to make the necessary changes. If towards the end of the project you still have few returns then you will have to do the best analysis that you can with what you have.

6.1.5 Not thinking about the data analysis before collecting it

Again, this is just bad planning and your tutor may have spotted this weakness in your project proposal. However, if this has happened then you may have a lot of disparate unconnected data that you are not sure how to handle. If this is the case, then it is essential to sit down with your tutor and identify a useful way forward. Whatever you have got, almost certainly something constructive can be done with it. It is just a case of getting the most value out of the resource that you have gathered.

6.1.6 Not enough time for writing up

This is another time management issue. The best way to guard against not enough time for writing up is to do the writing up as you go along. It means that at the end your time is spent editing and polishing rather than generating original text.

As time is the key, budget a specific amount of time each week, or if you are not good at this, each day, to be spent actively engaged on the project. Crudely, you can measure your output by using doing a 'word count' (found in the Tools menu of Microsoft Word) on your text. But . . .

> **Don't be fooled into thinking that quantity is quality.**

Alternatively, divide the time allocated to the project and dissertation by the number of days to the hand-in day. Treat the result as the minimum number of hours per day to be worked *every* day.

Time budgeting is a self-discipline tool that authors use. In preparing this book the issues of time, deadline and productivity were important.

However, if you find yourself short of time, and up against the hand-in deadline, then prioritise and focus upon the most important parts of the dissertation. It is true that all the parts are important but you should not compromise on the abstract, the conclusions and recommendations, and the analysis. But above all, make sure that the dissertation is handed in on time.

As one last desperate measure, you could try applying for an extension of time. Be aware that unless there are significant factors that have affected you and which were outside your control, such as a death in the family or your own serious illness, you are not likely to get much sympathy.

> **If, through bad planning or misfortune, you are up against a deadline, select and prioritise.**

6.1.7 Reporting literature without reviewing it

There are some students who, when faced with the task of writing the literature review chapter, manage to find some references on their chosen subject, but only extract information from those references without appraising them. For them, the task of critically appraising the references is either too challenging, or they do not understand what is required. If you find yourself in this position then go back and review Section 5.3.5.

> **Some find the process of doing a critical appraisal difficult. If you need to, seek advice.**

What you are trying to do is to evaluate the quality of each reference; in other words, you are giving a justified opinion of its usefulness in the context of your project and of its integrity. If you are still unsure of what is required, consult your tutor who may be able to point you in the direction of former students' critical appraisals in their dissertations. If dissertations are held in your institution's library you may be able to get some inspiration there.

6.1.8 Failure to analyse the strengths and weaknesses of the research

By the time you have got to the stage of writing the conclusions and recommendations chapter you will have the end of the whole task in sight. The temptation is to rush to completion and the sense of relief that brings. But now is the time to take stock of the whole project and one part of that is to critically appraise your own work. This is not just about confessing your sins of omission, but about analysing what went well and what went wrong and why, so that you and your readers can learn from your experience. You will get far more credit for giving an objective appraisal than you will lose by pointing out your own mistakes.

6.1.9 Writing it all up at the end of the project

A few students do this and suffer the consequences. If time becomes tight then write less, but still write well. An all-night session of writing to deadline at dawn is not to be recommended. The quality of what you write will be poor and you will probably not have time to check your work and so leave glaring errors and omissions in it. Your marks will reflect the quality of what you submit.

> **Quality cannot be rushed.**

 ## 6.2 Recovering from disaster

So you lost the original instructions for your project and got distracted by other but more immediate deadlines perhaps. The fieldwork was a disaster in that the weather was foul while you were trying to collect data and your friend who promised to help you suddenly announced that she was going on holiday. On return, when you tried to analyse the data that you did get, they utterly failed to fit the model that you had assumed so that you are now unable to draw any strong conclusions. Your flat was trashed by your so-called mates at last night's party and your paperwork is strewn across the floor. When you recovered your laptop from under the bed and set it up, the cat jumped in through the window and vomited over the keyboard, causing you to spill your coffee into the hard drive so that now it does not work at all. There are three days to the hand-in deadline.

A tale of disaster indeed, but can you recover the situation or are you going to fail your project entirely? Not necessarily, but it is going to take some concentrated work so you had better clear your social diary and focus on this task alone for the next three days. Obviously at this stage it is too late to go out and do more fieldwork so you will have to make the most of what you have got. So gather together what you can from the wreckage of your flat, clean the upturned pizza from the field records and dry out the beer-stained paperwork on the radiator.

> **You can usually recover from apparent disaster, but it will take some thought and planning.**

Since you have lost some of your data and the analysis of it did not go well, concentrate on presenting what you do have as well as you can. Even though your laptop no longer works, hopefully you have got some earlier, if incomplete, versions of other parts of your dissertation, either as printout or files sent by email or backed up on the institution's computer system, or on CD or another memory device. (You have been backing your work up regularly in a separate place, haven't you?!)

Recover what you can from this. Even with poor data, incomplete results and weak analysis you can still concentrate on the introduction and literature review chapters and the recommendations part of the conclusions chapter. Given the scenario above, there will be plenty of recommendations for further work that you can make. In spite of all that went wrong, make sure that you critically appraise your strengths and weaknesses. OK, the weaknesses will be easy to spot but there will be some strengths in there somewhere, so a little creative, but truthful, writing will be called for. You can also spend some time making sure that the appearance of the final document is good, especially the abstract.

Get some help with the paperwork.

If time really is tight consider getting some help with the typing. Can you call upon your flat mates, new boy/girlfriend, mum or favourite aunt? Since this is now a rush job it is essential to get someone else, not the typist, to read it for errors of logic, English, spelling and grammar. 'Spell-check' is a superb device for presenting you with a wonderful selection of alternative, but incorrect, words to choose from. Yes, it is tedious I know, but your tutor, being somewhat older, will have been brought up in a time when such things as grammar and spelling were more important, and will expect it from you.

● 6.3 How to make it go right from the start: prevention better than cure

The key word for getting it right is 'anticipation'. That is, anticipating what can go wrong and countering it before it can happen. Here are some ideas, in no special order, which may help you to make a success of your project.

6.3.1 Accept criticism

Attend all the meetings that your tutor calls you for. Regular meetings help to keep you focused, help you make quantifiable progress because you will need to have something to report at each meeting. They may help you to build up a rapport with your tutor which could have a positive, if subtle, effect when it comes to marking your dissertation. Keep the meetings brief and come prepared.

Criticism is normally well intentioned.

You will receive constructive criticism from your tutor, especially with respect to your written work. Accept it in the spirit in which it is intended. If the criticism concerns the conduct of your investigation and you profoundly disagree with it then you will need to have a very good reason for rejecting it and you will need to justify that reason in the dissertation.

6.3.2 Data

Decide on the data that you need and collect only those data. That of course means planning what you need to collect. Very seldom within science and engineering does it pay to collect everything that you can and hope to be able to sort it out and use it later. If you find yourself collecting spurious data it suggests that you need to go back and clarify your aim and objectives.

If you are doing a laboratory-based project, keep a notebook in which to record details of the experiments performed and the techniques you have used. Record your results and the references you have consulted. Note your conclusions and points you might develop in the analysis of the results. If yours is a software project then annotated listings of code may be useful. Your laboratory notebook may be required for assessment.

In your laboratory notebook you should date each page and head it with a title for the experiment, such as LB01. Make notes of procedures employed, apparatus or equipment used, consumables used and the order in which they applied. List the measurements taken in the correct units and with the appropriate number of significant figures. Draw diagrams of the apparatus, chemical reactions or processes. It may be useful to keep a digital camera handy. Keep a copy of any safety assessments or statements of safe working with the laboratory book. If you have kept proper records then anyone should be able to repeat the experiment just by reading your laboratory book.

6.3.3 House style

If you have been given instruction upon how to present your dissertation, follow it.

Write up using the house style.

It is unlikely that you will be penalised severely for small transgressions but if your dissertation looks radically different from that of your peers, your tutor will immediately be aware that you have not followed the instructions and you will lose marks accordingly. So if you have a house style, use it!

6.3.4 Independant cheque off you're typped werk

Did you notice the errors in the heading to this section; three wrong words used and three spelling misteaks, opps! and another. The trouble with these kinds of mistake is that they are so easy for you to make, but having made them, so difficult for you to spot. You tend to read what you expect to read. However, someone else is more likely to read what they see. So before you display your apparent incompetence or ignorance to your tutor, get someone independently to read your dissertation. Do not rely on the spell-checker to spot or even correct all your errors.

Sp ell c heck show's know err or inn this cent tense!

. . . but it is clearly nonsense as written (but makes sense if read aloud – 'spell check shows no error in this sentence'). Make sure you are using the correct version of the language by setting your spell-checker to the correct version of English. Microsoft Word has about twenty to choose from. British English presented in a US institution, or vice versa, will not go down well. Your tutor will know the difference and may take strong exception.

Box 6.1 Commonly mistaken words

Do you know the difference between the following?

advice advise, allowed aloud, all ready already, all together altogether, angel angle, a part apart, about around, assure ensure insure, auger augur, a way away, a while awhile, bare bear, belief believe, boarders borders, bought brought, brake break, breath breathe, buy by

capital capitol, choose chose, coarse course, collage college, complement compliment, contaminants contaminates, continual continuous, core corps corpse, council counsel, crevasse crevice, criteria criterion, cue queue, currant current

defamation deformation, defuse diffuse, deprecate depreciate, desert dessert, device devise, do due, disinterested uninterested, disassemble dissemble, drier dryer, dual duel, die dye

ecology environment, elicit illicit, eminent imminent, enquiry inquiry, ensure insure, fair fare, farther further, faint feint, for fore four, formally formerly, foul fowl, gild guild, good well, hangar hanger, heal heel, hear here, hole whole

incidences incidents, incite insight, install instil, jam jamb, jerry-built jury-rigged, former late, later latter, lead led, less fewer, liable libel, loose lose, mean median medium, miner minor, moral morale

naval navel, notate note, ordinance ordnance, passed past, patience patients, pedal peddle, personal personnel, perspective prospective, plain plane, pole poll, pore pour, practice practise, precede proceed, premier premiere, prescribe proscribe, principal principle, quiet quite, rational rationale, review revue, role roll, root route

sail sale, seam seem, shear sheer, sheaf sheath, sight site, soar sore, stalactites stalagmites, stationary stationery, suit suite, taught taut, their there they're, though thought through thorough, threw through, timber timbre, to too two, vain vane vein, wary weary, we're were where, who whom, who's whose, your you're.

Repeated mistakes can really annoy the reader so make sure you know the correct usage of common words. In recent years collective ignorance of the use of the apostrophe has come to the fore. Know the difference between cars, car's and cars' and, as contradictory as it appears, be aware that *it's* means *it is* and *its* means *belongs to it*. Other common errors include mistaking where for were, affect for effect, weather for whether (or even wether) and there for their. See Box 6.1 for some more commonly mistaken words. How many typos have you spotted in this book?

Checking is a tedious process so you could arrange with a friend to read each other's dissertations. Allow time for this; you will both be under pressure close to the deadline.

6.3.5 Interviews – be prepared

A lot of effort goes into setting up an interview. You need to identify who will be suitable to interview, persuade them to accept an interview with you and get yourself to the interview, so it makes sense to be prepared with your list of questions and issues that you want to explore. Before you go, reread Section 3.10.

6.3.6 Note taking

Make notes as you go, not just for references as described in Section 5.3.4. Jot down your thoughts, ideas and comments as they occur to you. If you do it on a computer you can possibly copy and paste sections of your notes into your dissertation. However, if you are going to do this it is imperative that you *do not* copy and paste into the file anything you have got from the internet or other source as you could inadvertently find yourself guilty of plagiarism if the internet text ends up in your dissertation.

> **Copy and paste may lead to unintended plagiarism.**

If you really must copy and paste from your computer, do it as a 'print screen'. That way you will be able to keep the record as a picture but will not subsequently be able to extract text from it.

A safer way of note taking is to use a hard-covered notebook. The advantage of a notebook is that it is easier to see all the contents at a glance than it is to see them on a computer screen.

6.3.7 Presentation

The presentation of your dissertation is important; allow plenty of time for this final stage. It will take longer than you think to collate and tidy up your written work. Make sure you adhere to any instructions about house style. If you share a printer, will there be a queue of others who are trying to get their dissertation printed at the same time? If you have to present your work in a specific form of binding only available at a particular shop, find out what turnaround time they can guarantee.

Above all, get it in on time to avoid penalties. If for some unavoidable reason you cannot get it in on time, discuss this with your tutor as soon as the problem becomes apparent; you might get some sympathy and even an extension of the deadline.

> **Telling your troubles to your tutor one day or one hour before the deadline will not get you far.**

6.3.8 Questionnaires

A project using surveys by questionnaire is not an easy option. Collect only that information which will enable your conclusions to be determined and no more. Keep the questionnaire as short as possible. Consider using a two-stage process, so first try out a pilot questionnaire and do preliminary analysis to make sure you will be able to draw useful conclusions. Think about sending an initial survey form with only one question asking if the company would be willing to participate and if so, the name of the contact person. Then send the full questionnaire to that person. Most people in commercial companies do not have the time or patience to complete long or complicated questionnaires.

6.3.9 Say 'thank you'

Saying 'thank you' is no more than common courtesy. If someone has helped you with their time or resources, let them know their help was valuable and appreciated. In being in contact with these people you have developed a number of potentially useful contacts that you might call upon when you are looking for a job or working in industry. A simple letter is all that is required, or failing that, an email or phone call. If your project is likely to be of interest to any of your supporters you could offer to send them a copy.

> **Thank you very much for all the help you have given me while I was doing my project!**

6.3.10 Start at the beginning

This might sound obvious, but having devised a question, aim and objectives, next concentrate on the literature search and review to find the state of knowledge in your project area. The results of this exercise might cause you to go back and revise your objectives or even the question and aim. If that is going to be necessary then it is best to do that before you get too far, for example with data collection.

6.3.11 Take regular breaks

Nobody can concentrate for hours on end, especially when hunched over a keyboard typing a dissertation. It is good to take your eyes off the screen regularly and also to rest your mind. You will know that it is time to stop when you find yourself engaging in 'displacement activity'. That is, when you find yourself doing things that, even momentarily, allow you to evade working at the task in hand. For example, unnecessarily sharpening pencils, watering house plants, repeatedly doing 'word counts' of your text, or looking for washing-up to do.

> **Cataloguing your CDs will not get the dissertation written.**

We all have our own favourite displacement activities and you will know what yours are. When you find yourself doing them you are becoming unproductive. A short burst of physical activity could be a good idea; a jog or a walk might help.

6.3.12 Write as you go

Not only does writing the chapters as you go make the writing process more manageable, but it is easier to write material at the time you do the work associated with it. Depending upon your relationship with your tutor, you may be able to get some feedback which, at the very least, will allow you to know you are on the right track, or to discover at an early stage what needs to be changed or developed further.

● 6.4 Summary

- Many things can go wrong if you don't guard against them.
- Avoid inertia; break the task into manageable parts.
- Size the task by selecting a sufficiently narrow and focused question. If you find that you have chosen too broad a subject to investigate, revise your aim and objectives.
- If you run out of time to collect or analyse data, reduce the data to be collected or simplify the analysis.
- Make sure you know how you are going to analyse your data before you start collecting it.
- If you run out of time while writing the dissertation then concentrate upon the high-mark-earning parts, namely the abstract, analysis and conclusions and recommendations chapters.
- Make sure you understand what is required of you for the literature review chapters. If you do not fully understand the concept of critical appraisal, consult your tutor.
- Make sure you analyse the strengths and weaknesses of your research. This will show that you are able to be objective and self-critical.
- Write up as you go; do not leave the writing up to one mad rush at the end.
- If everything does go horribly wrong, do not panic but concentrate on the parts that you are still able to present well. Short-term time budgeting will be called for. See if you can get help with the typing.
- It is better to anticipate and hence avoid problems than just react to them when they occur.
- Accept criticism; it is well meant.
- Collect only the data that you need.
- Follow the house style for writing up.
- Get a critical friend to check your typed work.
- Prepare for interviews to get the most out of them.
- Keep notes systematically as you go.
- Be careful of the quality of the final printed work.
- Politeness pays. Let everyone who has helped you know that their support has been appreciated.
- Put plenty of effort into the literature review in the early stages of the project. You might learn something that makes you refocus your aim.
- Take regular breaks when writing up; it will make you more productive and help to stop your text sounding as tired as you are.

What next?

Think about the rest of your project. Try to identify the places where things could go wrong and take actions to nullify their effect.

Anticipating problems will help you to avoid them.

Assessment and beyond

You have handed the dissertation in, but that is not the end.

The assessment process will vary from institution to institution, so what follows here is general guidance. As will be apparent by now, you should always follow your own institution's and your tutor's directions.

The assessment of your work may include more than just marking the dissertation. The project proposal, risk assessment, ethical review, preliminary literature review, progress presentations, progress reports or other written outputs may also gain marks. If that is so then you will need to allocate time and effort to all of these activities. There may also be marks awarded for your application, effort, industry or attitude during the project. Taken all together, their marks may amount to a significant proportion of the total to be awarded.

The aim of this chapter is to help you understand the overall assessment process so that you may improve your chances of gaining high marks. By the end of this chapter you should be able to:

- Understand the assessment process and how it may be applied at each stage.
- Prepare and deliver a good presentation.
- Understand how the dissertation will be marked.
- Prepare a paper for publication based upon your project.

7.1 Project proposal

In marking the project proposal your tutor will be looking to see that you have a viable project and that the evidence is presented logically. Providing that you have presented your proposal under the headings of: your details, title, rationale, question, aim, objectives, hypothesis, key questions, methodology, resources, structure of the dissertation, initial references, expected outcomes, work programme, as suggested in Section 1.4, then you should have logical structure to your project proposal.

Your tutor will then be looking to see that the rationale sets the scene for your question and that the question is sensible and answerable and that the aim derives from it. The objectives should fully support the aim without any of them being superfluous. If you have a hypothesis or key questions they should be necessary to the fulfilment of the aim and should not be unnecessary appendages designed to bulk out a potentially lightweight dissertation.

> **A good project proposal may earn you a significant number of marks towards your final score.**

In assessing your methodology, your tutor will be looking to see that your chosen method of capturing data will get sufficient and appropriate data. Your tutor will look to see that you have said how you intend to analyse the data and that the analysis will lead to the satisfaction of one or more of your objectives. You will need to show your tutor that the resources you have identified are reasonable, available and that you have access to them.

Your tutor will want to see that you have planned a suitable structure for your dissertation and that the list of initial references are cited elsewhere in the proposal, probably the rationale, and that they reflect a proper first reading of the subject area. The work programme will need to be reasonably detailed and indicate measurable milestones in the progress of the work. It cannot, for example, be just a list of proposed meetings with your tutor.

● 7.2 Preliminary literature review

If you are required to undertake a preliminary literature review your tutor will be assessing your ability to seek out, through the library, internet and other sources, relevant literature that covers your subject and to identify pertinent issues. What your tutor will really be looking for is to see if you have the ability to perform a critical analysis of that literature. Your level of technical knowledge and understanding will also be assessed.

One of the most common criticisms of literature reviews I find I have to make as a tutor is:

> 'This is a good review of the subject but not such a good review of the literature. You need to tackle this document the other way round. Start by identifying the literature associated with the subject area and then review it. You should be reviewing the literature by critical appraisal, not referencing a subject . . .'

● 7.3 Progress presentation and the viva voce

You may be required to give a progress presentation and/or you may be required to undergo a viva voce (Latin: live voice). If that is so, the key words here are preparation and performance, especially if your presentation skills are also being assessed. No actress will go on stage without learning her lines; no comedian will take the microphone without having his jokes prepared; failure to do so would mean being booed off.

> **Find out the details of any presentation you will be required to make so that you can be well prepared.**

To prepare, you will need to find out when the event is, where you are in any running order and what the format of the event is to be. The format for the progress presentation might be that you have to make a 10-minute presentation which outlines the aim and objectives of your project with a résumé of the outcomes so far, a description of what there is left to do and an assessment of the likely outcomes. There is likely to be a short question period at the end of your presentation.

Your audience might be your tutor and a group of your peers who could also be taking part in the assessment process. There may also be students from the previous year of your course whom your tutors are trying to inspire before they start on their own projects.

Your tutors might conduct a viva voce after the dissertation has been handed in and marked. The viva voce may itself be marked and the marks counted towards the final aggregate score or it may be that the purpose of the viva voce is to confirm that the dissertation is all your own work.

Sometimes the viva voce is used to confirm that the marks you have been awarded are fair. It may be used to moderate the dissertation marks if you are on the borderline between grades or if you are on the borderline between pass and fail. If you are well below a possible pass mark you might not even be invited to a viva voce at all. Your assessment panel may be your external examiner, your course leader, your project module tutor, the project tutor and your industrial tutor if you are a part-time student. It is likely that the question period after your presentation will be more substantial.

> **Whether a project presentation or a viva voce, find out what presentation aids are expected or permitted.**

You might only be permitted to use overheads on a projector or you may be expected to prepare a PowerPoint presentation. If the latter, find out if a computer and projector are provided and whether you are required to load your presentation beforehand from a memory stick, CD or your drive on the institution's server. Will you be permitted to use your own laptop?

> **Dress appropriately for the occasion.**

If you are scruffy or too casual you will give the wrong non-verbal signals to those who are assessing your presentation. Be professional; you will seldom be wrong with a suit and tie, properly tied, or something similarly formal if you are female. This is not the time to be cool to impress your mates. It is better to be over- rather than underdressed.

7.4 Preparing your presentation

Poor preparation will lead to a particularly poor performance. You need to know what you are going to say and how you are going to say it and you need to prepare your visual aids.

You do not need to write every word that you are going to say, but it might help to do so if you feel apprehensive about your forthcoming presentation. Pace yourself to about 120 to 180 words per minute so that you can easily be understood by a small audience. If you do write out a full script, do not be tempted to read it out at the presentation. If you read a prepared script, you will lose eye contact with your audience and so lose your audience's attention. A reading voice tends to be flat, monotonous and quiet so you are in danger of being a bore twice over. This paragraph has 140 words and so should take about one minute to deliver. Try it. It may sound very slow as you say it, but it will be clear.

> **Prepare a short list of key words as a cue sheet.**

So, having drafted your talk, extract the important points and write these in large clear text, of at least 36-point in size, on one side of a piece of A4 paper. Lay it flat on the table in front of you while you speak.

> # This is 36-point type.

You will then have a series of cue words you can glance at if you lose the thread of what you are saying. Better still would be to incorporate the cue words into your slides.

Your talk needs a structure. Start by briefly introducing yourself and the subject of your talk. Then take your audience logically through your material; rationale for the project, aim and objectives, methodology and problems encountered, summary of results and conclusions. That is five separate items. If you only have ten minutes in which to talk that is an average of two minutes per item. The challenge will be to edit what you could say to fit into the time available.

> **Prepare your slides and test them on a wall screen.**

Given that time is probably very limited, consider what visual aids you are going to use and prepare them. Avoid the use of a white- or blackboard. There are three reasons for this:

■ You do not have sufficient time to waste on drawing or writing during your presentation.

■ Unless you are well practised, it is actually harder than it looks to produce a professional-looking display quickly.

■ If you write on a board, you will need to turn your back on your audience and so will lose their attention.

> **Do not be tempted to keep talking with your back to your audience.**

This is because your voice will become muffled and you will have difficulty concentrating on talking and writing at the same time.

In preparing your visual aids, consider what your audience already knows. Some may already be knowledgeable in the subject, such as the tutor(s) who have marked your dissertation, others will not. Therefore it is wise to pitch your presentation at the level of the layman who is generally well educated in science or engineering. You have only a short period of time to get your message across so do not lose your audience in complexities; small details will not be relevant.

Design each slide to grab your audience's attention; make it interesting.

How many slides or overheads should you have? It depends upon what you have to show. As a general rule, in my lectures, I budget two minutes per slide; but that of course depends upon what is on them. With very simple slides you could have more. Making sense of a complicated slide can be difficult, especially if the speaker is talking at the same time.

Usually pictures are better than words. The speaker will probably be using different words from those on the screen and the audience will have to concentrate harder to understand the written and spoken words at the same time. Also, there can be so much more visual information in a picture.

Graphs are better than tables, both on screen and on paper, for the reasons stated in Section 5.6. Make sure the lettering on your illustrations is large enough to be read from the back of the room. What looks good and clear on the computer screen does not always looks so good on a screen on a wall.

> # Make sure the lettering on your slides is
>
> large enough to be read from the back of the room or your audience will not bother to read it.

There is a 'rule of thumb' that says that there should be no more than fifteen lines of text on a slide; if you can keep it to no more than five then so much the better. An audience will just refuse to read it if there are too many words. If you have too much text or too many illustrations on a slide, split the slide into two or more slides.

A short list of bullet points is one way to minimise text and to give you headings as prompts to make sure you do not miss any important points. However, too many slides which are just bulleted lists can be very boring. Perhaps have no more than two in a ten-minute presentation. Figure 7.1 shows an ill-considered use of bullet points – but does contain an important message.

Not only that, but your audience can read in their heads faster than you can read aloud so they will be annoyed if they have to wait for you to catch up.

Use PowerPoint transitions sparingly, and then only for a specific purpose, to give emphasis to a particular point. They can be really irritating and so alienate your audience.

> ■ Do not read the screen; the screen material should supplement your spoken delivery, not duplicate it.
>
> ■ Reading it suggests that you do not know your material and have little idea of what is coming next.
>
> ■ It is rude to turn your back on your audience and an insult to their intelligence to read to them what they can easily read for themselves.

Figure 7.1 Inappropriate use of bullet points

So, if you must use transitions, use the ones that allow you to read the text as it appears; 'appear' and 'wipe right' are good. Avoid the ones that make it impossible to read during the transition; 'fly from left', 'spiral', 'swivel' and 'zoom' are particularly difficult to read while the transition is in progress. Although each transition lasts for only a couple of seconds each, their cumulative effect could add up to as much as a minute of your limited time.

Remember that although you deliver one short presentation, your tutors probably have to listen to many, therefore you need to make yours stand out from the others. The key to a good set of slides is to keep them as bold and as simple as possible. The key to a good speaking voice is to create interest by varying your voice; without overdoing it, of course.

> PowerPoint   KISS – Keep It Simple
>
> Speaking   RSVP – Rhythm, Speed, Volume and Pitch

Having prepared your presentation on a computer, make sure you have a backup copy on CD or other memory device. Also have a copy of your slides on paper in case the projector fails; at least you will be able to talk about them.

If everybody else is going to use PowerPoint, consider an alternative medium for your visual aids. A continuous series of PowerPoint presentations can be mighty tedious to sit through. Overhead projector (OHP) slides can be prepared using PowerPoint and although you cannot have transitions with OHP slides you can probably switch all the lights on in the room. The change of ambiance will help to get your audience's attention.

A flipchart will look quite different, but of course you will not be able show any images that you have not drawn yourself. Make sure all the charts are fully prepared and look professional. You can always emphasise particular points by occasionally circling or underlining on the chart as you speak. The great advantage of a flipchart is that you are not vulnerable if the computer or projector fails.

Before you start, make the stage your own.

Position the lectern, table or other furniture where you want it. If you have a computer screen in front of you, you do not need to turn around to look at the screen on the wall; the images are the same. It may seem that an act of faith is required, but if by some remote chance the projector should fail, your audience will let you know.

If you think you might be nervous, take a sip of water before you step up on stage. If you feel the need to have water to hand while you speak, pour it into a glass or plastic cup before you start. Nothing looks worse than a speaker who stops to take a swig from a bottle.

Make sure that the lighting in the room is as you want it, with the maximum light available in the body of the room but with the screen on the wall not illuminated. If there is a white- or blackboard, clean it before starting your presentation. It will be very distracting for your audience if the previous speaker has left writing on the board, and you won't notice because you are facing your audience.

> **Get your audience's attention by making eye contact.**

To maximise the impact of your presentation you should try to engage eye contact for a few seconds with everyone in the room during your presentation. Not everybody feels comfortable about speaking in front of an audience, so if you cannot do this, make it look as if you are, by finding three points on the back wall at about the head height of the back row, and deliver your presentation to these.

Preparation, as we have said, is the key to a good presentation, so you will need to rehearse. Actors do it and so should you. There is a world of difference between preparing a presentation on a computer and presenting in front of a live audience. Start by standing and speaking out loud in the privacy of your own room. Once you are happy with that, get together with a couple of friends and deliver your own presentations to each other.

Make sure your friends tell you if you have any distracting physical mannerisms such as jangling keys in your pocket. If you are a jangler, empty your pockets before you start. Think what you are going to say and then say it. Do not be tempted to fill the natural pauses with 'non-words' such as 'um . . .' and 'er . . .'. Occasional pauses are good, even dramatic, but don't overdo it. They give your audience a moment to understand and appreciate the significance of what you have just said.

> **Take notes of what went well and what did not and give each other positive, helpful and constructive feedback.**

If you are well prepared you will be much more confident. If you cannot manage to rehearse with friends you can always fall back on the most critical audience you will ever have: deliver your presentation to the bathroom mirror.

Finally, know your slides and present them smoothly. Talk freely, confidently and enthusiastically; after all, it is your subject and you will know a lot about it. If you enjoy talking about your chosen subject, then your audience will enjoy listening to you.

Best of luck – and have fun!

● 7.5 Poster presentations

An alternative to the 'stand-up' presentation described in the last two sections is the poster presentation. Delivering a poster may be less intimidating but will probably require more work. A poster presentation is obviously more than just an abstract but much less than the full dissertation.

The first thing to find out is how your poster will be staged. What are to be its physical dimensions? Is the aspect landscape or portrait? Landscape is easier to read because the audience will not have to look high up or low down, but a landscape poster takes up a greater length of wall space. Will it be printed as a single large document or will you have to put it together from individual pieces of A4 paper stuck to a backing card? Is there a standard format that you will have to follow or will you have free rein for your design?

Will your poster be hung in a room with all the others for your tutors/examiners to view at leisure, or will you be in attendance and expected to answer questions and engage in discussion with the examiners? If it is the former your poster will have to stand alone and be self-explanatory; if the latter your poster does not have to contain so much information and you will have the opportunity to develop your ideas in conversation.

Your poster will contain much the same information as a stand-up presentation. The main difference is that in a stand-up presentation you control the delivery of that information, whereas in a poster presentation it is the audience who select what information they take and what they ignore and also the order in which they read it. If your poster guides your audience through the information in a logical order then it is more likely that they will read all of it.

> **Create something eye-catching as well as informative.**

Remember, however, that the message is more important than the medium in which it is delivered.

The background should enhance the text, not dominate or obscure it. The background might be white, a plain colour, a graphical design, a photograph or a montage. The text should use no more than two fonts throughout and it is best to select fonts that are easy to read and have an authoritative appearance, such as Times New Roman, Arial or Veranda. If the text is to go directly onto the poster then the background should be pale and unobtrusive. If the text is to be in panels with their own backgrounds then the overall background can be more striking. Have fun designing the background but do not spend too much time on it. Simple and less is usually better than more.

A bold banner heading should go at the top. It should have a short, concise and self-explanatory title, the same one as your dissertation, which can easily be read from 5–10 metres away, with your name slightly smaller perhaps, below it. I suggest font sizes of 72 and 48 respectively. You may be given a template to follow.

> **The text of your poster should summarize the main parts of your dissertation in an easily readable and eye-catching way.**

You could lay the poster out in sections with arrows taking the reader from one section to the next.

As with a 'stand-up' presentation, focus on the main argument, results and conclusions only. The text should be easily readable from 1–2 metres so font sizes around 20 would probably be best. Each section should have a clear heading; likewise, any photographs, graphs, tables or other illustrations need clear captions.

Your poster should start with an abstract and this may be the one from your dissertation. The first text panel should explain your rationale for the investigation, the nature of the problem that needs to be addressed, your aims and objectives, the scope of the investigation and the limitations of your work. You should be able to find all this information from the first chapter of your dissertation.

The next panel should describe your methodology, followed by a panel presenting the main results. You may have a few associated tables, graphs or photographs. Next there should be discussion of those results (the analysis) followed by a panel with your main conclusions. If your text contains references (only have the most important references, not all of them) then a references panel will be appropriate.

Having selected the material that is to go on the poster, focus on the layout. You could have images interspersed with text as in Figure 7.2 or you might get a more

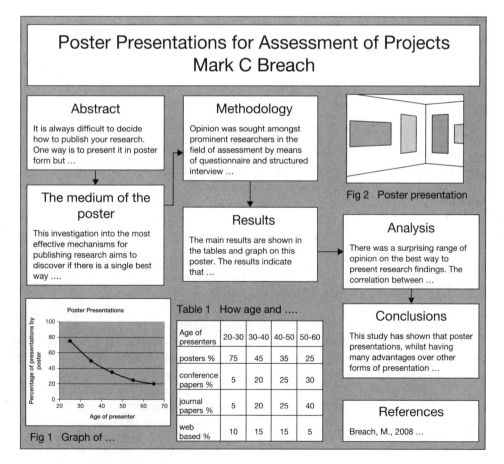

Figure 7.2 Poster presentation layout

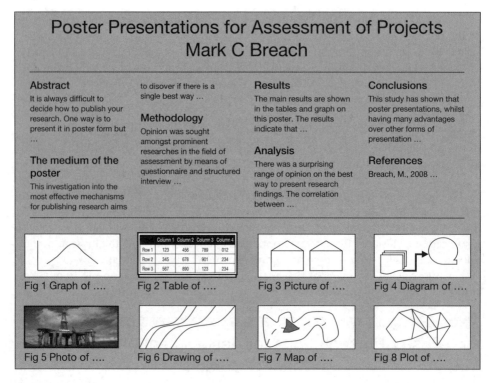

Figure 7.3 Bottom-aligned poster layout

ordered appearance if the text is in one box with the images right- or bottom-aligned as in Figure 7.3.

Now compose your poster by sketching on a piece of paper, which is the same shape as your poster will be, boxes for images and for text and then label each item.

Each section should have a header in a larger font size and in bold format. Break the text into short paragraphs for easy reading (as in this book) with a line spacing of 1.

Figure 7.2 shows a possible layout for a poster presentation. Obviously, on one page of a book it is not possible to show all the detail of a poster that may be printed on A0 sized paper.

● 7.6 Marking the dissertation

The method of assessment of your dissertation will vary from institution to institution. One possible model is that your tutor and another tutor will mark it separately. No two people will evaluate the merits of the same piece of work in exactly the same way. A difference of opinion is to be expected; marking is not an exact science.

If the assessment is within a certain percentage, say 5%, then the final mark may just be taken as the aggregate of the two. If the disagreement is not greater than 10%, say, the tutors may discuss their assessments with a view to coming to an agreed mark. If they cannot agree, or their disagreement is greater than 10%, then a third tutor may be appointed to resolve the deadlock. It is likely that your external examiner will also see parts of your dissertation though would not normally be involved in its marking.

Electronic submissions can easily be used to detect plagiarism.

If you are required to make a submission as a DOC or PDF file then the chances are that your tutor will be testing your dissertation for plagiarism; see Chapter 8 for details. It may also be that your work will be archived in this form.

What your tutor is looking for has been described in the previous chapters, especially Chapter 5. To gain high marks you will have to show that you have a comprehensive understanding of basic principles associated with the subject of your project and that you can apply those principles in a creative way to solve a specific problem.

You will need to show that you are able to analyse and evaluate the issues concerned with a question, in a logical manner. In science and engineering there is usually some mathematics or some laboratory work or fieldwork involving calculations. If so, then it should be complete and there should be no errors, or at worst only very minor inaccuracies that do not affect the validity of any analysis or conclusions.

All your work should be presented according to the instructions you have been given, and written in concise, clear and correct English.

Any drawings, pictures, graphs and tables need to be neat, clear and appropriate. If you have made assumptions in your project, they will need to be clearly stated and justified.

Your tutor will be looking for written evidence of wide and appropriate reading as part of your literature review and throughout your dissertation. All sources need to be correctly cited and listed in the reference list.

On the other hand, you risk not even passing if you show a superficial understanding of the fundamental principles or if your mathematical and numerical work is incomplete and inaccurate. Likewise poor English will let you down, especially if English is your first language.

Every course in every institution will have a different template for marking your dissertation and it is not possible to include all of them here. Box 7.1 shows one possibility.

To make sure your dissertation is not wanting in any respect, it is a good idea to find out how it will be marked.

If you are a part-time student and have an industrial tutor, it is possible that your industrial tutor will have difficulty knowing how to mark your dissertation. You can help by giving your industrial tutor a copy of any instructions you have been given and by putting your industrial tutor in contact with your academic tutor.

7.7 Preparing for publication

Now you have handed in your dissertation and it has been marked. To your relief, and possible amazement, you have been given a good mark. What next? You may have something which, with a little editing, could be turned into a publication. In Section 2.2 the reasons stated for doing this were that it will look good on your CV and will also give you some exposure to industry and to your potential employers. Academic careers are built on publications, if that is the way you see your life progressing.

Box 7.1 A marking scheme

Project proposal (10%) Clearly identified and defined aims, objectives, hypotheses and key questions.

Methodology of the investigation (15%) Choice of method with justification. Appraisal of the methodology, design of data collection and analysis.

Literature review (25%) Search and identification of relevant literature. Critical appraisal of the literature. Demonstration of scientific or engineering knowledge and understanding of the project topic.

Implementation (25%) How the methodology was applied to the collection and the analysis of the data. The appropriateness and completeness of the data collection and analysis.

Analysis, conclusions and recommendations (15%) Presentation and interpretation of the data. The strength and relevance of the conclusions. The appropriateness of the recommendations and scope for further work.

Written presentation (10%) Ability to follow the instructions for the written work. Succinctness. Structure, organisation, written style, grammar and spelling.

You are now writing for a different audience.

In editing your dissertation, think of your chosen audience, i.e. the readers of the journal to which you will submit your paper, as it will now be called. The best way to see the style of papers in your target journal is to read a few recent copies. You will need to reduce your dissertation to about six to a dozen pages for a refereed journal and considerably less for a professional journal. Make your submission attractive to the editor by following the style of the journal closely. It will only be published if the editor, and possibly reviewers appointed by the editor, like it. Don't be put off by this; most editors will be sympathetic, up to a point, with young and first-time authors.

Choose the journal with the subject area that most closely fits the subject of your dissertation.

Somewhere in the journal or on its associated website there will be an 'instructions to authors' section. Read this carefully before you start editing, and then read it again when you have finished, to make sure that your submission fits exactly with what is required. Box 7.2 shows an abbreviated example to indicate the general style. Most 'instructions to authors' will contain more detail. Some journals require that you produce 'camera ready' copy. If this is the case, the content and layout must conform exactly to the journal's house style because the final copy you submit will be scanned as it is and reproduced in the journal.

After you have submitted your paper to the editor you will probably receive a brief letter, post card or email acknowledging receipt. It will then go quiet for two or more

Box 7.2 Example instructions for authors

Instructions for authors

Send four printed A4 paper copies – for the editor and each of the three referees. Send a copy of the submission as an email attachment with the text in Word format (DOC) and also all graphical figures and photographs as separate files in JPG format.

Keep your own original on disk as a backup.

Print double-spaced on one side of the paper only. Use Times New Roman or Arial; 12-point in size. Include all tables, figures and reference list. Margins are to be at least 2.5 cm top, bottom and both sides. Figures may only be black and white or greyscale. The textural layout of the paper copies must be similar to the style of the journal. Figures and tables should be placed within the text and must have suitable captions. References are to be in the Harvard system.

The title must be concise, reflecting the subject of the paper. It is to be followed by the name(s) of the author(s) and their place(s) of work. Give an abstract and at least four, but no more than seven, keywords. The main body of text follows.

Instructions or comments for the editor must be bold and in red to show they are not part of the text.

Paper copies must be unfolded and the pages stapled together.

Papers when printed should not normally exceed 16 pages in length, including references, figures and tables. The text will not normally exceed 5000 words in length.

The editor will inform authors of the comments of the referees to aid revision of the submission by the author(s).

If the paper is accepted for publication, proofs in PDF format (for typographical correction only, not revision or amendment) will be emailed to the lead author only. Proofs must be returned within 72 hours of receipt.

All submitted material must be the author's original work which other publishers are not currently considering.

By submitting, authors confirm that the work does not infringe any copyright and will compensate the publisher for any consequential loss if it is found to do so. Upon publication, the authors assign legal copyright in the submission to the publisher unless agreed otherwise.

months during the peer review process. It is likely that the editor will read the abstract and scan the rest for obvious flaws before sending it out. Once again, notice the importance of the abstract. The editor will be looking for a clear structure to the paper, correct citation and referencing as well as a readable narrative style. The first impression will tell the editor something of the care with which a manuscript has been prepared.

Either here, or after peer review, you will receive one of the decisions shown in Figure 7.4.

A conditional acceptance is usually as good as it gets. Even the most accomplished academics very seldom get an outright acceptance from the top-ranking journals.

There are many reasons why you might get a rejection or be asked to revise and resubmit. Before you submit it is worth checking that none of the reasons in Figure 7.5 might apply to you.

Outright rejection. Bad luck; perhaps you sent your paper to the wrong journal. Think if you could do better elsewhere. If you get some feedback, consider it carefully.

Rejection, but with encouragement to revise and resubmit. If this is the case you should get some feedback to help you to do this.

Conditional acceptance. This is good so be very encouraged. Read the feedback and make the necessary amendments and resubmit.

Outright acceptance. If this should happen, start working on your next paper; you obviously have both ability and flair.

Figure 7.4 Editor's decisions

Imprecise description of your data sample

Insufficient detail about your methodology

Introductory section that does not clearly present the issues

Invalid statistical analysis

Irrelevant citations for your topic

Muddled research question

Overlong or too short

Poor English

Too much or too little literature review

Unnecessary discussion that has little to do with the research question, a particular problem if you are editing down a dissertation

Vague description of the topic

Weak discussion of the results

Figure 7.5 Reasons why papers may be rejected

Once you have completed your paper, put it away for a few days before reviewing it yourself. Since you are likely to have to revise your work, it is worthwhile spending some time to minimise that task. You can check your work at three levels (Figure 7.6).

Since this is probably the first time you have submitted for publishing, it is a good idea to get a colleague or two who have published before to read it. Their experience may enable them to spot any issues that need to be resolved and so increase your chance of publication.

How to check your paper

Level 1 Make sure that the paper presents your arguments and discussion as a coherent whole, from abstract to reference list.

Level 2 Next, do likewise for each paragraph for reading style and delete any unnecessary words and phrases.

Level 3 Finally check each word for spelling, punctuation, grammar and usage.

Figure 7.6 Checking your work

> **In the discussion section of your paper it is often a good idea to talk about the unexpected results you have achieved, with some discussion of why that might be and what might have happened if you had conducted your investigation differently.**

Part of the process of turning a dissertation into a paper is one of selection. Your dissertation will be too long as it is, so you need to select only those parts that make a coherent whole, and dispense with all the peripheral arguments, data and analysis. You will almost certainly dispense with your appendices. If you have copied anything from other sources then that must go as well. If you have a long list of references then that should be edited down to only those that are pertinent and recent. In doing so, of course, the same rule about listing a reference for all citations and citing all references still applies so you need to be careful about editing your text. Remove all references to unpublished work. In evaluating your paper for publication the editor and reviewer will also be looking at the quality of your writing.

7.8 Copyright

You may think that as you have written your dissertation, and it really is your own work, you own the copyright in it. Beware, that may not be the case. Your institution may insist that you transfer copyright ownership in your dissertation as a condition of being allowed to submit it for assessment.

If you were required to sign a declaration to that effect then the position is clear. Even if that was not required of you, there may be something in the institution's regulations that state that the copyright has been transferred. Obviously this is not a serious issue if you do not intend to publish, but if you do, you will need to get the institution's agreement or risk possible legal action by your institution and publisher.

7.9 Summary

- Reread Section 4 of Chapter 1 to ensure that you have a logical structure to your project proposal.
- If you undertake a preliminary literature review, your tutor will assess your technical knowledge and understanding as well as your ability to perform a critical analysis.
- The literature review must critically appraise the literature as well as identifying its contents.
- The key words for your viva voce and progress presentation are preparation and performance.
- Prepare and test your slides on a screen in the room in which you are going to do your presentation.
- Write out the main headings of your talk.
- Rehearse your presentation in front of colleagues.
- Clean the board, adjust the lights and set the stage to your satisfaction.
- Plan on two minutes per slide.

- Graphs are better than tables. Use big text on slides and the less text the better.
- One or two bullet point lists only. Use PowerPoint transitions sparingly.
- Face your audience and engage eye contact.
- Consider if you can prepare a paper for publication based upon part, or the whole, of your dissertation.
- Be prepared to select and edit ruthlessly.
- You may need to amend your submission after it has been reviewed.

What next?

Find out from your tutor how your dissertation will be assessed.

Find out where and when your presentation or viva voce is to take place and its format.

Write up your dissertation as a paper for publication.

Plagiarism – avoidance and detection

You will know what cheating means.

Possibly you have been tempted; possibly you know others who have done so and you probably know what would happen to you if you got caught. Cheating is when you try to advance yourself by some means that works against the normal ways that your knowledge, abilities or skills are assessed.

Your institution will take cheating in examinations or in coursework very seriously and there will be severe penalties for doing so. As a result of a particularly bad case, a student could be thrown out of the institution. If someone else cheats, it is you who are being cheated, because the cheater is devaluing your degree. If you cheat, you are doing the same to everybody else.

The aim of this chapter to help you understand the nature of plagiarism and so avoid compromising the value of the work you have done. By the end of this chapter you should be able to:

■ **Understand what is meant by plagiarism and why you must not do it.**

■ **Understand how you are likely to be caught if you do plagiarise.**

■ **Develop a strategy to avoid plagiarising accidentally.**

You will almost certainly be required to confirm in writing that the work you present is original and your own. You are required to do this for a reason; it is so that the institution can take action against you if the declaration turns out to be substantially false. There is an example in Figure 8.1.

8.1 What is plagiarism?

Plagiarism is a form of cheating. You would be guilty of plagiarism if you tried to pass off someone else's work as if it were your own.

Declaration of Originality

I declare that this is all my own original work, except as declared in the citations, references and acknowledgements. The work is not the product of plagiarism, collusion, fraud or any other academic irregularity. The dissertation and the original work related to it have not previously been submitted to any institution for an academic award.

Signature: Name: Date:

Figure 8.1 A declaration of originality

> **Plagiarism is intellectual theft.**

There are many ways in which plagiarism may take place. If you copy some text from a book or journal and incorporate it into your work you will be guilty. If you copy from a friend you will also be guilty. It does not matter whether your friend allowed you to make the copy, it would not affect your guilt.

If you allow a friend to copy your work you will be guilty of collusion and your institution will probably take just as dim a view as if you had committed the act of plagiarism yourself. Therefore you would be very unwise to lend your work to a friend or even get someone else to hand your work in for you. It is better not to lead others into temptation as you may be blamed for their sins.

> **The most common form of plagiarism is that of copying and pasting from the internet.**

It is so easy to do and so many do it because they think that they can get away with it. That may have been true in the past but it is no longer so, for the reasons explained in Section 8.3.

You may not realise that it is still plagiarism if you paraphrase some text you have found elsewhere. Merely changing the order of the words and replacing some of the words with others of similar meaning is still plagiarism. It is simply because you would have taken someone else's ideas, their intellectual property, even if you have rearranged their words.

It is still plagiarism if you take someone else's ideas and present them as your own. If you attribute them in the correct way that is fine, but by not attributing them you are, by default, claiming them as your own. See again Section 5.4 on citing references.

Sometimes it is essential to quote a section of somebody else's text. You should do this sparingly. Do too much, or do it too often, and it will look like padding, which it probably is. Consider first if a normal citation will work just as well. Really the only time you need to quote directly is when you have to discuss the words that are used in the quoted text.

Here are two examples of using quoted text. In Figure 8.2 the text has been quoted correctly and in Figure 8.3, if this was your text, it would be pure plagiarism.

The text being quoted in Figure 8.2 is in italics. This way of quoting another author's text is correct because it is cited in the writer's own text and the quoted text is in quotation marks. To avoid a charge of plagiarism the absolute minimum that it is

There are various ways in which the relative positions of the stars may be viewed. Breach (2004) states:

> *'Just by looking at stars, planets, Sun or Moon you can have no idea how far away they are, indeed they all appear at the same distance, but of different size and brightness. If we work with the stars and other celestial bodies as they appear to us rather than as they are, we can introduce the idea of the celestial sphere. With this concept we can put ourselves at the centre of the sphere and give our celestial bodies two-dimensional celestial coordinates based on their apparent positions on that celestial sphere. Spherical coordinates are something we sailors are already familiar with; we describe our position on the water in terms of latitude and longitude.'*

In this approach Breach reduces a three-dimensional system to two dimensions and relates it to the coordinate systems familiar to the reader. The advantages are . . . but . . .

In the reference list:

Breach, M.C., 2004. Celestial Navigation when your GPS fails. Crewe: Trafford.

Figure 8.2 Correctly quoted text

There are various ways in which the relative positions of the stars may be viewed.

Just by looking at stars, planets, Sun or Moon you can have no idea how far away they are, indeed they all appear at the same distance, but of different size and brightness. If we work with the stars and other celestial bodies as they appear to us rather than as they are, we can introduce the idea of the celestial sphere. With this concept we can put ourselves at the centre of the sphere and give our celestial bodies two-dimensional celestial coordinates based on their apparent positions on that celestial sphere. Spherical coordinates are something we sailors are already familiar with; we describe our position on the water in terms of latitude and longitude.

In this approach one can reduce a three-dimensional system to two dimensions and relate it to the coordinate systems familiar to the reader. The advantages are . . . but . . .

Figure 8.3 Incorrectly quoted text

necessary for you to do is to put the quoted text in quotation marks and to cite the source.

Notice how the quoted text has also been put into italics, a blank line left above and below and the quoted text indented to the right. This makes it absolutely clear that the passage is not the writer's but that it is being quoted from another source.

Now compare Figure 8.2 with Figure 8.3.

The middle paragraph of Figure 8.3 is pure plagiarism because there is no citation of the publication that it has been copied from and the copied paragraph is not in quotation marks. If you had written this, a reader would assume that the middle paragraph contained entirely your own ideas in your own words.

Not many students understand about plagiarism when they start their course and therefore initially may have the excuse of misunderstanding what is required. However, by the end of your course, your tutors should have made the institution regulations and practice very clear to you and so any plagiarism will be treated as academic misconduct.

● 8.2 Why people plagiarise

So why do students plagiarise? There is a changing culture in education. When your tutors, and their tutors, were at university there was greater competition to get a place and so most students valued the opportunity and were there to learn and understand. The degree that came at the end was of less importance. Now a greater number of students take the attitude that the learning is just the work that has to be done to get the qualification. Some are therefore tempted to take the shortest route to getting that qualification without worrying too much about the rules.

There are a number of excuses that students put forward for plagiarism; some seem almost logical until you examine those reasons more closely.

> Anyone who puts stuff on the internet is just asking for it to be copied.

Not true. People make material available on the internet for a variety of reasons. That material is not yours for you to claim as your own. Not only are you committing an act of plagiarism by copying it un-attributed but you may also be guilty of a breach of copyright.

> The reference I found said exactly what I wanted to say; I can't think of a better way of putting it.

Maybe, but someone else has already said it, not you. So if you want to quote it then you must cite the source, list the reference and put the segment that you use in quotation marks.

> OK, I copied it from the internet into my computer; but now that it is in my computer it belongs to me.

No, it does not. You may have acquired a copy of the text or even a whole file. Whether the physical file now belongs to you does not matter here; the intellectual property contained within it certainly does not. If you use the file or the text without citing it and putting the quoted part in italics you are guilty of plagiarism.

> I did not know about plagiarism.

'Nonsense' is the response you are likely to get. Your institution, through your tutors, will have warned you all about it. You may have to make a declaration that your submission is all your own work when you submit coursework. And of course you have read this book, so you have no excuses for ignorance.

> I did not have enough time.

So, you are owning up to being disorganised as well as being a plagiarist?

> I thought I would get better marks if I copied good quality material.

It is up to your tutors, of course, but the chances are that you got no marks at all, as well as getting yourself into trouble.

> In my last institution everybody did it and the tutors did not mind.

Possibly so. In some cultures around the world that is true, but your present institution will take a very different view of plagiarism!

> It was so easy to do.

And now just as easy for you to get caught.

> I am paying for my degree so it is up to the institution to provide all my learning materials.

If you are paying, it is for the opportunity to study for a degree, assessed by normal methods. As part of your study you are required to use your own initiative and effort.

> I thought I would get away with it.

Well, did you?!

8.3 How you are likely to be caught

Tutors have always been aware that material has been copied. It is usually easy to spot suspect material in a student's submission. The difficulty has been in proving plagiarism because to prove it, it would be necessary to track down the original source document and then make a line-by-line comparison. As this often involved a lot of work with no certainty of success, some of the less conscientious tutors would turn a blind eye to obvious plagiarism in the past.

Some tutors view blatant plagiarism as contempt of the tutor by the student.

It is the student's way of saying, 'I think that you, the tutor, are so dumb that you cannot see when I have copied another person's work'. If the student is right, the tutor will spend more time reading the plagiarised work than the student spent doing the 'copy and paste'. Nobody likes to be taken for a fool so you can expect little sympathy from your tutor.

Many papers in professional or academic journals appear in edited or expanded forms on websites. Some students do not realise this and think that plagiarism with an optical character reader cannot be easily traced.

8.3.1 Indicators of plagiarism

Before looking at why you will almost certainly get caught, let's consider some of the obvious indicators that tutors look out for.

The student's work appears to be of a substantially higher quality than expected. Your tutors will know quite a lot about your abilities by now. If you have been having difficulties just getting pass marks and then you produce a dissertation containing the scientific insight of Einstein and written with the literary flair of Shakespeare, your tutors will be very suspicious.

In plagiarised work there are often changes in the quality of English. This is especially easy to spot with students whose first language is not English. Students whose first language is English but who also find difficulties with writing are also unlikely to be able to see the telltale changes of quality.

When other people's work is incorporated into your own there are significant changes of style. Different people write in different ways. For example, you will have noticed the deliberate style of this book, much of which is written in the second person singular; that is, it is written by the author as if speaking directly to you, as in this sentence.

If you copy a web page you are also likely to copy the formatting. Suspicion is aroused if there is an unexpected change of font, text size, character, colour or justification. 'Copy and paste' with unformatted text will solve most of those problems but will create others; for example, formatting that you intended to carry over will be lost so that, for example, $e = mc^2$ in the original text will appear as e = mc2.

> **Spot the error . . .**
> **'If a body accelerates uniformly then the final velocity is related to the initial velocity by the formula $v22 = v12 + 2as$'**

. . . where of course it should have been $v_1^2 = v_2^2 + 2as$.

If an author writes in US English and then you copy the text into an otherwise UK English dissertation (or vice versa), the American spelling, grammar or usage will stand out. Your tutors, who probably have more experience of written English of various forms, will easily spot the anomalies.

There are many other ways of spotting plagiarism, but since I am also a tutor who assesses students' dissertations, I am not going to give all my secrets away here. Your tutors will almost certainly be aware if you have done a significant amount of plagiarism.

Figure 8.4 The Turnitin website

8.3.2 Plagiarism detection service

Finding and proving plagiarism used to be a long and difficult process, but no longer. The plagiarism detection service used by most institutions, at least in the UK, is Turnitin, which may be found at www.submit.ac.uk. See Figure 8.4. Turnitin works by comparing a file submitted by your tutor to the database of existing web pages, archived web pages, and previous submissions to Turnitin. At the time of writing, the database consists of over 9 billion items including 50 million previous student submissions. Turnitin accepts up to 250,000 essays each day, is used by 6,500 institutions world-wide, including almost all UK universities.

Upon receipt of your piece of work Turnitin prepares an 'originality report' consisting of the text of your document with the sections where it has found common text with other sources highlighted. Not only that, but the web address etc. of the source is given with a listing of all the sources, with the percentage of your document that is common with each of the other sources. Sections of your text that are in quotation marks may be excluded from the detection process. An overall statistic of non-originality is given and this may be used as a first indicator of the incidence of plagiarism.

Almost every document will contain some element of apparent non-originality.

For example, every dissertation submitted to me will have the words 'Dissertation submitted to the Nottingham Trent University for the degree of . . .' on the title page. See Figure 8.5. Clearly this would not be considered plagiarism and so would be ignored. There will always be phrases that crop up in common usage and phrases that are specific to a particular area of science or engineering. A single phrase in isolation could hardly be used as evidence of plagiarism.

However, when full sentences, especially from the same source, occur, suspicions are aroused. A complete paragraph highlighted in a non-originality report would normally be taken as conclusive evidence of plagiarism.

The non-originality report would normally be examined to confirm that all the substantive highlighted text really is what it appears to be. In other words, your tutor will examine the evidence to be sure that it is watertight if it is challenged.

Since there will always be some apparent plagiarism in any text, what percentage of non-originality would be construed as proof of plagiarism? Even the most plagiarism-free documents will probably show 1–2% of non-originality. Depending on the context of your document and your use of technology-specific jargon, it is rather unlikely that a document that is truly free of plagiarism will have more than about 5% of non-originality. Anything greater than 10% would be treated with a good deal of suspicion. Consider the evidence for plagiarism in Figure 8.5.

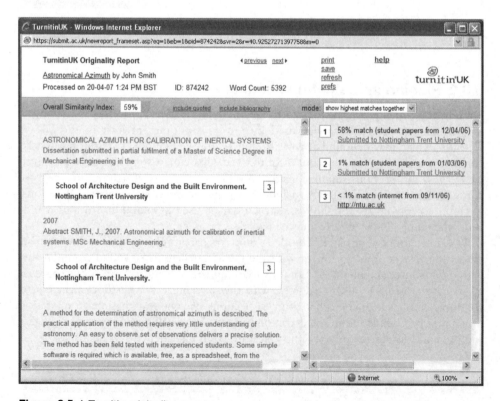

Figure 8.5 A Turnitin originality report

8.3.3 Beating the system?

Some students like to believe that they can beat the plagiarism detection service by editing their plagiarised text. Rearranging the order of sentences, paraphrasing text, using a thesaurus to change one word for another may bring down your overall non-originality score by a few percent. However, a score of 35% is just as damning as a score of 40%. In practice it would be easier to write the dissertation correctly in the first place rather than waste time trying to massage someone else's text. It is just not worth the time and effort and risk if you fail to fool your tutors.

You may think that if you copy material from a book or a journal it cannot be traced.

You would be unlucky if your tutor had read the same material before. However, if someone else has previously copied the same material and the dissertation or course-work has been submitted to Turnitin then that material will be in the Turnitin database. If you now present the same material, your work will be shown to be unoriginal because of someone else's plagiarism. Poetic justice indeed!

There are a number of websites that claim to employ someone who will write your dissertation for you. Advertised costs are from around £10/$20 a page of 200 words. If you are expected to produce a dissertation of 20,000 words using such a service it would cost you about £1000/$2000. Such a dissertation cannot contain anything of a personal nature that links you with your apparent investigation and would be extremely difficult to defend since there is nothing of yours behind the text.

Some websites claim that your dissertation will be written by an MSc or PhD from a university. A simple check on the professed credentials is likely to show that the university claimed is in fact bogus, i.e. nothing more than a 'degree mill' that gives degrees based entirely on self-certified experience. Such degree-awarding activity is illegal in the UK but not illegal in some other countries.

Those authors have various tricks they employ to try to make the work look authentic. Sometimes they use fictitious citations to make the text look scholarly. Such citations may fool the idle student commissioning the work, but if your tutor decides to follow up a reference like:

Smith, J., (1999) Scientific methods in dental engineering, Journal of education in engineering science, Vol. 27, pp 123–132, London: Nowchester Publications.

it won't take long to discover that no such paper, journal or even publisher exists.

Paying someone else to write your dissertation is likely to be money down the drain as well as leading to a failed degree.

8.4 What happens when you get caught?

What happens when the inevitable occurs rather depends upon your institution. Having gathered the evidence, your tutor will put into action the formal processes prescribed by your institution. You will probably be confronted with the evidence such as the

Turnitin report or the material that you have plagiarised and be invited to admit the plagiarism.

If, in spite of the overwhelming evidence against you, you still deny the offence, then a hearing chaired by a person who is independent of your tutors will probably be convened and the evidence of your plagiarism will be presented. A report of the outcome will go to your board of examiners who will decide what action to take. If it all gets this far, it has also got very serious indeed and you would be advised to seek help or representation through your student's organisation. Serious cases of plagiarism may lead to expulsion from your course and you may fail your degree.

As a projects tutor at both undergraduate and postgraduate level I am always saddened when I have to 'prosecute' a case of plagiarism. On the other hand, I have never 'lost' a case.

● 8.5 How to avoid accidental plagiarism

Now you, as an honest student and having read the foregoing sections of this chapter, may be concerned that you could be severely penalised for something that is really not your fault.

> **As an honest student you have little to fear; your tutors are not out to trip you up, but they are on the look out for the serious plagiarist.**

What you need to be careful about is accidentally incorporating reference material into your text. When compiling notes it is better to keep all your material in printed form rather than as files on your computer so that you cannot be tempted to 'copy and paste'.

When you are typing your work, do not have your references open beside your computer. It is easy to be tempted to write the same phrases or sentences that you have just read. It would be much better to read your references, making brief notes as you do so, and then, with the references put away and out of sight, use only your notes as a reminder of the pertinent arguments when writing your dissertation. Make sure to include your thoughts and evaluation in the text. Of course, you must still cite your references correctly because, although the words may now be your own, the ideas and arguments have come from other sources.

● 8.6 Summary

- Plagiarism is a form of cheating; it is intellectual theft. It is trying to pass off the work of others as if it was your own.
- The penalties for plagiarism are severe.
- Do not lend your un-submitted work to others.
- If you quote someone else's text, make sure you cite it properly and put the quoted section in quotation marks.
- Students plagiarise for many reasons. Do not be tempted; none of the reasons are valid.

- If you plagiarise you run the risk of being caught. There are many ways in which you give yourself away if you copy another's text or ideas.
- Your tutors probably use a plagiarism detection service such as Turnitin. This has taken the hard work out of proving plagiarism.
- If you are required to submit your dissertation as a computer file, it is very likely that your dissertation will be tested for plagiarism.
- Do not be tempted to try to beat the system; you will most likely fail.
- Do not pay others to do your work for you; it will almost certainly be money and a degree wasted.
- Be careful that you do not accidentally plagiarise. Keep any notes in paper form rather than as copied internet documents on your computer.

What next?

There is very little in this box because the chapter was primarily about what you should not do, rather than what you should do.

However, it is worth checking your dissertation to make sure that you have put any direct quotations into quotation marks and that you have cited each reference correctly.

Make sure that each citation in the text is backed by a reference in the reference list and that each reference in the reference list has a corresponding citation in the text.

Hand in your dissertation on time.

Best of luck!

CHAPTER
9

Questions and answers

Here are some real questions that my students have asked me about projects and dissertations. By reviewing the concerns of some former students you will appreciate that you are not alone in having questions, and you may find some of the answers you seek here. Although the range of subjects is fairly limited, the answers address general points that could apply to almost any subject area in science and engineering. My answers are in *italics*.

Q1

I don't have an exact title for my project as yet but wanted to look into waste management on site. I've researched, mainly on the web and a browse through the library, but think there may be an area that I can look into. My belief is that waste disposal is not taken seriously on site and no real thought is put into this area of a project. I would like to research into whether there are more effective and efficient waste disposal techniques than just shipping all the waste to landfill sites which are forever increasing in price to use. I think that in the future the cost of waste disposal will be at such a significant level that contractors and project managers will have to start thinking about it more seriously and allocate more funds to this area of construction. These are just a few issues but there are external factors affecting this situation also, such as government legislation and EU directives involving construction waste material that will eventually force all in the industry to think long and hard about the best way to deal with their waste! Do you think this is a viable proposal for a project?

This sounds an interesting area to investigate. So now you need to focus in on what will be your research question to answer; what are the most effective methods of waste disposal on the construction site perhaps, your aim, objectives, methodology etc. Could this have a working title of 'Future waste management on the construction site'?

Q2

I've been thinking about my dissertation subject and wanted to know what you thought about the following: 'The economical and environmental impacts of over-engineering slopes'. Aims are to compare the factors of safety of slopes constructed of the same material but with different gradients. Then look at the costs involved with use of additional materials, plant and transport of material to site.

An interesting subject but there should be only one aim. A single well-focused sentence is required. So would the aim (singular) really be: to investigate the environmental and economic impacts of safety of slopes constructed of the same material but with different gradients.

'Investigate' would be better than 'compare'.

In addition to the economic costs, I would look at the environmental impacts such as quarry-limited natural resources, carbon emissions from earth-moving plant and transport.

Sounding a bit woolly, what are you really proposing to do?

This would probably be based on hypothetical slope designs with computer analysis of slope stability.

If this is to be a desk study using software, can you validate your conclusions with real-life case studies?

Q3

I propose to undertake my dissertation along the lines of investigations in determining the feasibility of reusing existing foundations for a new development. Something along the lines of 'The aim of this project is to investigate the load-bearing capabilities of existing foundations for newly constructed or refurbished buildings'. I am not aware of any publications covering this subject.

Regarding the 'research' part of the dissertation, however, I propose to utilise techniques used in other industries. Such techniques include x-raying (beneath floor slabs), blasting inside buildings and using video probes, for example, which, as you can appreciate, are not generally used in geotechnical investigations. I assume I will not be penalised by using existing techniques.

This sounds interesting. I suggest a slight change of aim to: 'The aim of this project is to investigate new techniques for assessing the load-bearing capabilities of existing foundations for newly constructed or refurbished buildings'.

You say there are no publications on the subject. Is this a new subject that has not been addressed by anyone before? If so, then there is lots of scope for originality. There must be publications relating to the techniques you propose to investigate in their non-geotechnical applications. How will you assess them in the context of geotechnical investigations, i.e. have you thought about the methodology? Are there any case studies you can draw on? Will you be conducting any trials yourself?

Q4

My interest is to investigate the effects of construction on the environment, in particular global warming and the benefits of waste management. I have not yet begun any research but wanted your opinion on the subject as well as any other guidance you can offer at this stage.

You have identified a broad area of interest which sounds appropriate. The next step is to narrow that area down so something much more focused and specific and therefore achievable in the limited time you will have available. Having done that, the next step is to devise a question that you seek the answer to.

Q5

I have found a company that will help me with my project. We are in talks at the moment to see if there is any research that would benefit them and that I could undertake for my project. It would be an advantage for me as I would be researching something completely new; I would be able to get data from them as well as first-hand experience.

In principle this sounds good. The advantages are as you state, as well as networking leading to a job perhaps, if you like each other.

But beware of compromising objectivity. It is hard to elaborate on that one without knowing the project you have in mind but it could be related to conducting a biased investigation leading to conclusions slanted to what the company wants to hear. Bias could come about by investigating the product or process that the company is proposing to the exclusion of alternatives from other companies.

But don't get hung up by this; it is just that you must keep an open and objective mind and a little intellectual distance from the company when conducting your investigation; no doubt if they have any knowledge of the research process they will understand this.

Make sure that the company understands that your dissertation will end up in the public domain (if only through submission to Turnitin); it cannot be made confidential.

Q6

Just a couple of queries regarding the use of and referencing of figures.

If a source has granted permission to publish a figure in its original form, is this a breach of copyright? For example, permission has been gained for figures obtained from Defence Estates and the UK Climate Impacts Programme. Is it necessary to redraw these figures?

If it is a direct copy the source and the ownership need to be acknowledged with something like 'reproduced from Bloggs (2008), by kind permission of Defence Estates . . .'.

If a figure has been created in its own right, i.e. not simply redrawn, but based on information (data) from various sources, how should this be referenced?

The figure is your own but you must state where the data have been gathered from.

Q7

I'm mid-way through completing my dissertation. How many pages does it need to be?

How long and how deep? You may have noticed that I am always reluctant to give word counts. Thoroughness and quality are better measures. The answer is as many words as you need and definitely no more.

Q8

The title for my dissertation is: 'Trees considerably increase the severity of single vehicle accidents within Derbyshire'. It is a subject where no previous research has been carried out and there are no present requirements to protect trees from the possibility of a vehicle colliding with them. The reason I chose single vehicle accidents is that where there are other factors involved in the accident (i.e. another vehicle) then the other factor is likely to affect the severity of the accident and so it would be hard to judge what effect on severity the tree has had.

The title you suggest sounds more like the conclusion, and therefore you already have the answer to your problem. Remember, you start with a question like: how do trees affect the severity of single vehicle accidents within Derbyshire?

   This sounds an interesting area of study but it seems to me that there will be much thinking required to put together a satisfactory project proposal for this one. Some questions come immediately to my mind. How many single vehicle accidents involving trees per year are there in Derbyshire? Is there enough data for your study? How will you separate out the effect of the tree in each accident?

Q9

I have chosen three possible titles for my final year project. I would be grateful of your comments on the suitability of each:

An investigation into how production line technology/methods can be used for the prefabrication of residential buildings.

Building self-sufficiency using renewable energy sources and recycling.

Advances in safety measures and development in the design of rollercoasters.

The titles all look fine, but a title is just a title. You need to think through the aim of the project, the objectives that need to be accomplished to satisfy the aim and the methodology, i.e. how you are going to do it. However, at this stage the most important decision is which of your proposed investigations will generate the most enthusiasm for you. And do you think it will be viable given what you know of the subject already?

Q10

My proposed title is: 'Engineering principles and techniques for the prevention of flooding'. I've thought long and hard and feel this is a subject that can be greatly expanded and investigated whilst keeping me interested. Over the summer months I can do further research to decide exactly which field I want to concentrate on, whether it is to investigate building on flood plains by analysing case studies to show how flooding could have been prevented or to investigate how global warming may affect the way we build in the future etc.

Sounds like this could be interesting once you have narrowed down the field of your proposed investigation. The next step is to think about exactly what it is that you intend to investigate, find a research question, and decide how you propose to go about the investigation.

Q11

I am considering two different types of project and I seek your advice on which one to pursue.

Project 1 – Tunnel induced settlement of piled foundations

The project would rely on two case studies from the newly built Channel Tunnel Rail Link (CTRL).

Only two – could be a bit limiting perhaps.

The aim would be to compare the settlement of the bridge with the settlement of the ground.

The aim needs to be more along the lines of: 'to investigate the interrelation between the settlement of ground and bridge . . .'.

There have been quite a few studies on this type of project so I could compare the results with other results and theories.

That sounds more promising. Is this a live investigation? Will you collect original data? Will this involve measurements for deformation monitoring?

Project 2 – Permeation grouting of terrace gravels to increase skin friction on piles

The project would rely on field trials and tests carried out to show that permeation grouting of terrace gravels below a piled foundation would reduce settlement of a bridge caused by the construction of a tunnel (again CTRL).

So if this is what you expect to find you should try to show the opposite.

The data have been analysed to show how much of an increase was produced by the grouting but no research has been carried out to explain or quantify the increase. An initial literature review reveals that there have not been many studies in this area. There are not very many results but I think there are enough to produce a valid project.

Be sure your project is more than just a literature review; it should be an investigation to answer a question.

Q12

Is there any guidance on how to write acknowledgements?

Acknowledgements usually follow the main text, on their own page. Ensure that the titles of companies and people are correct. In the acknowledgements only, you can use Dr or Prof.;

but never use Mr; initials or Christian names are acceptable. Personal titles are never used in the main text. But keep it brief, factual and not obsequious. Consider if you really need to do so at all.

Q13

The deadline for the submission of a project title is approaching and I have come to a point where I am quite stuck. I have done what was required but I think I am still missing the killer title. I have got a number of ideas, the majority of which fall under the category of Tunnelling. I was wondering if you could have a look at them and give me some advice on the direction I should be heading or which one sounds the most feasible.

Tunnelling advancement in relation to the consumers needs in the 21st century.

Construction of tunnelling for higher train speeds.

The reliability of tunnelling construction in earthquake zones.

Construction design for the expansion of the London underground system for the London Olympics.

Environmental implications of widening the M25.

Each of these could be a project. A title does not tell me all that much. Some of them are rather broad and need to be narrowed down to something more manageable in the time you have available. So now take each one and find a research question to answer, then find the aim and decide what the objectives are, i.e. things you need to do to satisfy the aim, and then consider your methodology, i.e. how you are going to do it. You will probably find that some of your ideas now look less practical and hopefully one jumps forward as the obvious winner.

Q14

How about this for a dissertation topic??

An investigation into the differences in construction between steel and concrete framed buildings, including an investigation into the relative construction programmes, the benefits of each type of construction, the cost of each type and the particular requirements to initiate each construction type.

You have identified a subject area but I cannot see a clear research question here. Is it something to do with cost/benefit analysis of different construction types?

The subject area looks too broad to get anything meaningful in the limited time you have available – we need more focus. You could achieve that by applying constraints to the investigation, such as limiting the geographical location to Europe, England or Nottinghamshire perhaps. Limit the type of building to residential or commercial, its maximum and minimum size, the nature of its purpose or the maximum and minimum contract values. Are there other constraints?

Just an idea I was having that might benefit me in the industry I plan to go into. I really don't want to pick a topic off the list because I think I will get on with it better if it's out of my own head.

Yes – good for added value and motivation.

Q15

I am thinking about doing a project on 'Tactile mapping for the blind'. Are there any special issues I need to think about?

You need to be aware that if you intend to interact with blind people, e.g. interviews or testing, this project will require ethical assessment and ethical clearance. This is unlikely to be an onerous task, but it has to be done; you will not be permitted to proceed without it. (Note that to proceed with your project without doing so could be a university disciplinary matter.) It all starts with completing an ethical assessment form. The form is several pages long but most of the questions are of the yes/no type.

Index